THE
80/20 INDIVIDUAL

THE
80/20 INDIVIDUAL

HOW TO BUILD ON THE 20%
OF WHAT YOU DO BEST

RICHARD KOCH

CURRENCY

DOUBLEDAY

NEW YORK   LONDON   TORONTO   SYDNEY   AUCKLAND

To Matthew

A CURRENCY BOOK
PUBLISHED BY DOUBLEDAY
a division of Random House, Inc.

CURRENCY is a trademark of Random House, Inc., and DOUBLEDAY is a
registered trademark of Random House, Inc.

First published in Great Britain and the Commonwealth by Nicholas Brealey Publishing as
THE 80/20 REVOLUTION.

THE 80/20 INDIVIDUAL was first published in the United States in hardcover by Currency
in September 2003.

Book design by Fearn Cutler de Vicq

The Library of Congress has cataloged the hardcover edition of this book as follows:
Koch, Richard, 1950–
[80/20 revolution]
The 80/20 individual : how to accomplish more by doing less—the nine essentials of
80/20 success at work / Richard Koch.—1st US ed.
p. cm.
Originally published: The 80/20 revolution. London : Nicholas Brealey Pub., 2002.
Includes bibliographical references and index.
1. Creative ability in business. 2. Executive ability. 3. Organizational effectiveness.
4. Time management. I. Title: Eighty-twenty individual. II. Title.
HD53.K625 2003
658.4'09—dc21
2003043753

ISBN 978-0-385-50975-6
Copyright © 2003 by Richard Koch
All Rights Reserved

First US Edition: September 2003
First Currency Paperback Edition: April 2005
All trademarks are the property of their respective companies

Contents

PART ONE

Turbo-Boost Your Career:
Become an 80/20 Individual! · 1

1	How to Be an 80/20 Individual	3
2	The Rise of the Creative Individual	13

PART TWO

The Nine Essentials
of 80/20 Success · 29

3	Use Your Most Creative 20 Percent	31
4	Spawn and Mutate Great Ideas	45
5	Find the Vital Few Profit Sources	65
6	Enlist Einstein	83
7	Hire Great Individuals	95
8	Use Your Current Company to Your Advantage	115
9	Exploit Other Firms	135
10	Secure Capital	149
11	Make Zigzag Progress	163

PART THREE

The 80/20 Revolution · 173

12 From Capitalism to Individualism   175
13 What If?   189

APPENDIX

The Roots and Ramifications
of the Revolution · 205

Notes and References   225
Acknowledgments   235
Index   239

PART ONE

Turbo-Boost Your Career: Become an 80/20 Individual!

CHAPTER 1

How to Be
an 80/20 Individual

Take away our twenty most important people,
and I tell you we would become an unimportant company.
—*Bill Gates, chairman, Microsoft*

Introduction

This book is about a revolution that is changing the lives of individuals, individuals who are changing the world. I call these revolutionaries "80/20 individuals," people and small teams who use the 80/20 principle to build businesses and fuel their careers. You may already be an 80/20 individual without knowing it, but if you are not, you have everything to gain by becoming one.

The 80/20 Principle, my earlier book, struck a chord with many readers by answering two questions:

❖ How can I use the 80/20 principle to raise the profits of my corporation?
❖ How can I use the 80/20 principle to be more effective personally?

This book answers a quite different question:

❖ How can I use the 80/20 principle professionally, to create my own wealth and improve my well-being?

This is a book for *individuals at work*. I explain how *you can become much more successful in your career* by transforming any business. Whether you are an entrepreneur, a manager, an executive, a worker, or unemployed, you can use the step-by-step method described to re-model an existing business or create a new one—one that most bene-fits *you and your close associates*. My objective is to help *you* first, your customers second, and corporations only if helping them helps you.

The world belongs to individuals, not to corporations. And by us-ing the 80/20 principle to accomplish more by doing less, you can turbo-boost your career.

A Brief History of the 80/20 Principle

In 1897, Italian economist Vilfredo Pareto (1848–1923) noticed a reg-ular pattern in distributions of wealth or income, no matter the coun-try or time period concerned. He found that the distribution was extremely skewed toward the top end: A small minority of the top earners always accounted for a large majority of the total wealth. The pattern was so reliable that Pareto was eventually able to predict the distribution of income accurately before looking at the data.

Pareto was greatly excited by his discovery, which he rightly be-lieved was of enormous importance not just to economics but to so-ciety as well. But he managed to enthuse only a few fellow economists. Although he could write lucidly on less momentous subjects, his ex-planation of the "Pareto principle" lay buried beneath windy academic language and dense algebraic formulae.

Pareto's idea became widely known only when Joseph Moses Ju-ran, one of the gurus of the quality movement in the twentieth cen-tury, renamed it the "Rule of the Vital Few." In his 1951 tome *The Quality Control Handbook*, which became hugely influential in Japan and later in the West, Juran separated the "vital few" from the "trivial many," showing how problems in quality could be largely eliminated, cheaply and quickly, by focusing on the vital few causes of these prob-lems.[1] Juran, who moved to Japan in 1954, taught executives there to improve quality and product design while incorporating American business practices into their own companies. Thanks to this new at-

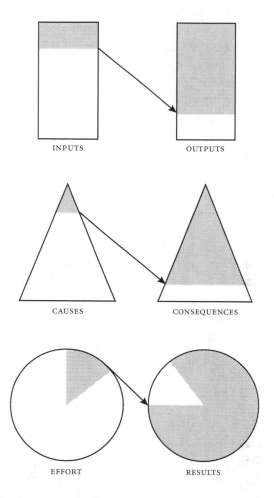

FIGURE 1: The 80/20 Principle

tention to quality control, between 1957 and 1989, Japan grew faster than any other industrial economy.

In the United States and Europe in the 1960s, the Pareto principle became widely known as the "80/20 rule" or "80/20 principle." While it is not wholly accurate, this description was snappy and influential. Engineers and computer experts began to use the principle routinely.

The 80/20 principle is an empirical "law" that has been verified in economics, business, and interdisciplinary science. It states that 80 percent of results flow from 20 percent of causes. In other words, most of what exists in the universe—our actions, and all other forces, resources, and ideas—has little value and yields little result; on the other hand, a few things work fantastically well and have tremendous impact. There is no magic in the 80 and the 20, which are merely approximations. The point is that the world is not 50/50; effort and reward are not linearly related.

Most of the universe consists of meaningless noise, which can drown out those few forces that are tremendously powerful and productive. But if you isolate and harness those powerful, creative forces within and around you, you can exert incredible influence.

In 1997, I wrote *The 80/20 Principle*,[2] the first book on the subject. I showed how the principle could be applied not merely to help corporations drive business results, but also to help individuals improve their lives. I explained how to become effective or happy by realizing the importance of just a few isolated people or things. If you concentrate on the few that work best for you, you can get what you want. You can multiply your effectiveness, and even your happiness.

This idea broke new ground, since nobody had previously linked the principle to individual fulfillment. It struck a chord; as many readers around the world discovered, the 80/20 principle is an extremely useful way to get more out of life.

This new book, however, has a very different theme. *The 80/20 Principle* showed how companies could use the "law" to drive business results and how people could use it to improve their personal lives—but not their professional lives. *The 80/20 Individual* demonstrates that the 80/20 principle is liberating and powerful, a practical business tool that individuals can use to increase their output and creativity in every aspect of their business and career. The link between the application of the 80/20 principle and an individual's role in creating wealth is one that has never been made before.

Value Comes from Growth

The most interesting and valuable part of business is not the maintenance of existing operations: doing efficiently today what we did yesterday, in the same way we did it yesterday. If every organization maintained the status quo, the economy would never grow.

Growth is more important. Growth means creating something new and valuable. Growth is ultimately driven by individuals and small, self-selected teams of individuals, operating both within established corporations and in new ventures.

The most formidable weapon for growth in business is the 80/20 principle, creatively applied by individuals and small teams of individuals. With the 80/20 principle, people can leverage the most powerful forces around them—tangible, but especially intangible ones—to dazzle the world and provide customers with much more of what they want for much less of what they wish to conserve (money, resources, time, space, and energy).

80/20 Individuals in Organizations

Individuals are usually only partly aware of what they could do to create wealth. They may also be unaware of what they are already doing. In this book you will encounter several people who are creating enormous wealth for others, without realizing it. They are already 80/20 individuals, but they are not yet reaping the rewards appropriate to their creativity. They think they are cogs in a corporate machine, while in reality they are at the heart of wealth creation and economic growth.

Even if you work for a large or prestigious organization, if you create something that reflects your individuality and your ideas, then *you* are the primary wealth creator. Usually, your corporation keeps most of the wealth that you create. However, once you realize the disparity between the value you create and what you get back, you can narrow the gap.

Those who can create wealth—and know that they can—are able to dictate their own terms. Wealth is a means to happiness, but it is not the main one. What most people want is control over their lives. They want the ability to choose how they live: what work they do, the way they interact with friends and colleagues, the quality of their personal relationships, the way they view themselves.

What you gain as an 80/20 individual is the right to control your life: your work life, your personal life, and the intervening spaces where they collide or mesh. For example, your understanding of the 80/20 principle can allow you to strike a completely different deal with your current employer.

Many 80/20 individuals can be partly inside and partly outside their organizations, retaining contact and continuity with colleagues while also embarking on side ventures. For many 80/20 individuals these hybrid arrangements are greatly superior to the traditional alternatives: either staying put and being exploited as an employee or starting a new business from scratch.

My premise is simple—if you add great value to your organization, know that you do, and can demonstrate how, you can reasonably insist on setting your own agenda, goals, and rewards because you will always be creating more value than you receive. If this simple view upsets existing arrangements with your employers, quit. So much the worse for them. You create—you are in control.

The 80/20 Principle Is at the Heart of Creation

People think that creativity is largely a matter of talent, experience, or luck. They are wrong. Talent, experience, and luck are all key elements, but there is something more fundamental, accessible, and powerful that you can use to multiply your creative effect.

The 80/20 principle is central to all acts of creation. Take plant growth. Rain is clearly important. And what causes rain? Clouds—but only a few clouds create the most rain, and only at particular times, in particular locations.

Fertile land is also important. While also partly due to rain, there are other factors that influence fertility, including the variety and number of plants and animals that have used the land before. As a result of small differences in these few factors, a few pieces of land will be tens of times more fertile than others, yielding stronger, healthier plants in greater abundance. In plant growth, as in all creation, a few key variables can make all the difference.

In business the 80/20 principle is behind any innovation, any extra value. It is an entrepreneurial principle, a formula for value creation utilized not only by entrepreneurs, but by most managers and organizations.

The human need for better value, higher productivity, and reduced effort is nothing new. It's what led humans to three of the greatest breakthroughs to affect our planet: the invention of agriculture, the agricultural revolution, and the Industrial Revolution. These conscious acts of creation vastly increased our planet's population and raised our standard of living.

How do such extraordinary conscious acts of creation happen? I could describe them in many different ways, but every conscious creation shares the following three characteristics:

Creation is a matter of rearranging things that already exist. "There is nothing new under the sun," as the Preacher said in Ecclesiastes.[3] The invention of agriculture around 7000 B.C. involved taking what already existed in nature and rearranging it to make it dramatically more productive. The agricultural revolution after 1750 rearranged the ancient elements of production, applying the leverage of scale and machinery. Scientists today study the processes of nature, then either speed up or alter the original process. An example is the microchip. Sand has existed in abundancy, with little value, for millions of years; yet a microchip, made of silica, formed from sand, can be extremely valuable.[4]

Conscious creation leverages the most powerful forces available. There are countless natural forces, both organic and inorganic. Only a few of them are really useful for creation. And within each species or type of force, a small minority are much more powerful and useful than the rest. Among all plants, a few vegetables are the most nutritious. Among farming methods, a few yield the greatest harvest. Among all areas of production, a few are the most efficient.

Breakthroughs in productivity occur when the most productive way of doing something is further enhanced by increasing scale or capital, or applying an innovative technique. These breakthroughs spring from thought and experimentation, the most powerful forces of conscious creation. Great things are created not only by the most powerful physical forces, but also by the most powerful ideas.

Creation occurs when ideas and individuals collide and collude. Of course, the raw materials of creation are physical, the stuff the universe makes available to us. But the essence of creation is intellectual.

The idea for the microchip did not arise from building sandcastles, but from building upon ideas. Creation requires ideas and individuals, usually only a few of each. All great scientific breakthroughs can be traced to a few fertile ideas that are pondered and rearranged by an individual or a small team. All business growth arises in the same way. Doing something differently, creating something new—all such actions start with an idea. The idea normally originates with an individual and is refined within a small team.

Business creation has a fourth common characteristic. If it is to survive, even for a time, **a business innovation has to improve value to customers.** It has to offer more for less—a lower cost or a better product or service—to customers who will pay for it. (It is not enough to offer something that is better and cheaper than something else if no one wants it, or if there is already an even better alternative.)

Both agricultural revolutions—the one around 7000 B.C. and that around A.D. 1750–1850—provided better food at much lower cost. Any automobile bought today costs a fraction of the price, adjusted for inflation or earnings, that it would have cost fifty years ago, yet cars today are much safer, faster, more comfortable, and more powerful. We get much more for much less.

Creation is not a mysterious process, confined to the scientific genius, the mad inventor, or the entrepreneur. Creation can be engineered, if you understand what drives it. Individuals and ideas drive creation. It happens in predictable and repeatable ways. If we understand this, we can create.

Become an 80/20 Individual

The 80/20 principle enables anyone who is determined, bright, and hardworking to stamp a footprint on the world by becoming an 80/20 individual. To make something new and popular, to feel that you have achieved something, and to acquire the status and freedom that come with this new territory—these are things to relish. In *The 80/20 Principle*, I explained how to transform your organization's performance and your life. In *The 80/20 Individual* I will show you how to use the 80/20 principle to create wealth, and improve your well-being by keeping part of this wealth for yourself.

CHAPTER 2

The Rise of the Creative Individual

Give me a single place to stand, and a lever, and I will move the Earth.

—Archimedes

The world has never before presented such ripe pickings to the individual creator. Whether you stay within your current firm, start a new one, or become a one-person adventurer, you can create things that other people want. And if you do *that,* you can gain control of your destiny.

I challenge you to create more—much more than you have before, and much more than you think possible. There is a powerful way in which this can be done, if you know how. To create something new and valuable you must express your individuality and tap into one of the most powerful forces on earth, the 80/20 principle. You must become an 80/20 individual.

The Rise of 80/20 Individuals

Business and society are being transformed by the fall of the collective and the rise of the individual—the 80/20 individual—as the source of both wealth and well-being. In this 80/20 revolution, capitalism is being replaced by a new, twenty-first-century form of team-based individualism.

80/20 individuals apply their individuality to create something new and useful to other people. They are not machinelike drones who maintain the status quo; they don't build machines so that the collective institution is more important than the individual.

80/20 individuals and teams are mobile. Their primary loyalty is to themselves and their small team of other individuals, not to an institution. They may build large and valuable organizations, but they know that the organization is there for the creative individual, not the other way around. The institution is their vehicle, not their master. Above all, 80/20 individuals are idiosyncratic individualists. Although they are lone individuals, they can have a profound impact.

Who Are 80/20 Individuals?

80/20 individuals cut across all established categories. They are found in all walks of life: in politics, business, social work and not-for-profits, sports, entertainment, the media.

Oprah Winfrey is an 80/20 individual. So are Jeff Bezos, David Bowie, Richard Branson, Warren Buffett, Jim Clark, Bill Clinton, Larry Ellison, Bill Gates, John Grisham, Andy Grove, Tom Hanks, Robert Johnson, Michael Jordan, Nelson Mandela, Ronald Reagan, Steven Spielberg. In her time, Florence Nightingale was an 80/20 individual. So were Christopher Columbus, Henry Ford, Isaac Newton, George Orwell, Mother Teresa, Sam Walton. Each of these individuals is known for more than his or her name. Each originally set out to do one job, to establish one career, but, in the end, all created something far greater—an entire enterprise based on them and their ideas.

Oprah Winfrey, for example, is not just a TV personality following an established format. She has created a *new* way of relating to viewers, and turned herself from a broadcaster into a businessperson. She has created trust between herself and her viewers. She has become her own *brand*. If she decided to never make another public appearance, her TV slots would be filled, but because she adds something novel and unique to our lives, *she* would be irreplaceable. In small ways or large, the same is true of all 80/20 individuals.

By contrast, those who inherited and run the world's organizational machines—armies, states, business organizations—and who did not create or transform them, are not 80/20 individuals. The UK's Queen Elizabeth, for instance, is not an 80/20 individual. Neither are Gerald Ford, Al Gore, nor, despite his popularity, George W. Bush. Most of the world's powerful but faceless people are not 80/20 individuals. Their power is organizational, not personal. They are interchangeable, part of an elite, not individual creators.

80/20 individuals create, and that is why they matter. Not because of their title or formal role, but because of what they do, because they are individuals, not part of a machine.

All successful entrepreneurs are 80/20 individuals. Entrepreneurs use their individuality to create something new and different and valuable. Thus, people outside business could be called entrepreneurs—artists, scientists, writers, broadcasters, stars of sport and screen, creators of popular movements of all kinds.

In business, however, the word "entrepreneur" is often misused, because creation in business is not confined to entrepreneurs. Many creative executives in large organizations create huge value as individuals, more than many entrepreneurs. One of this book's important themes is that creative executives nearly always get shortchanged by their organizations. My mission is to encourage such individuals to capture a large chunk of the value they create. If enough creative executives do so, the nature of the economy will change—from revolving around capital to revolving around individuals.

Creative Individuals Change the World

John Maynard Keynes, probably the twentieth century's greatest economist, recognized the pivotal world of creative individuals and personal optimism in creating growth and jump-starting economic revolutions. According to Keynes, the enemy of growth is perennial underinvestment. Because people are risk averse and the future is uncertain, there is rarely enough investment. Economic leaps forward occur when for particular reasons—such as the influx of gold from the New World or inventions like the steam engine—individual businesspeople feel unusually confident and expansive.[1]

We can apply Keynes's insight more broadly. Creative individuals literally change the world. Christopher Columbus's discovery of the Americas directly and indirectly created enormous wealth and allowed Europe to lead the world for nearly four centuries. The great scientists—Isaac Newton, Charles Darwin, Albert Einstein—expand and change our mental horizons, shifting our view of the universe and its potential. Individual entrepreneurs—Andrew Carnegie, Henry Ford, Bill Gates, Konosuke Matsushita, Akio Morita, or Sam Walton—transform whole industries. But the process can be jerky and lumpy as we wait for these rare creative people to push us forward.

Individuals and their small teams drive progress. Yet behind the flowering and proliferation of individual genius lie two neglected but vital conditions. One is what Keynes called "animal spirits," the feeling that the universe is a playground that we have barely started to explore. The other is the widespread application of one scientific insight: the 80/20 principle.

Creative Individuals and the 80/20 Principle

Think of all the billions of people in the world, today and throughout history. Now think of the number of people who have had a significant impact on the world: great thinkers, religious leaders, explorers, soldiers, scientists, politicians, artists. Whatever list we make, there is a very small number of people we can name who have made a significant impact on our daily lives.

Probably fewer than 1 percent of people have exerted more than 99 percent of influence on the world. These creative individuals have changed what went on before and what would have happened without them. And they have done so not as part of a mass, but as individuals: people taking a divergent view, thinking or doing something that would never have been thought or done collectively.

Would a council of religious leaders have originated Christianity or Islam? Would all the rulers of Europe have decided to sponsor a voyage across the Atlantic to find new lands? Would committees of scientists have decided that the world was round and not flat, or arrived at Newton's laws of motion, Darwin's theory of evolution, or Einstein's laws of relativity?

No one has ever quite understood the process by which individuals create. In this book, I present a new theory based around the 80/20 principle. It is obvious that creative people generate value that is many times greater than what the average person contributes. The mathematics behind the 80/20 principle suggests that the minority of creative people each produce at least sixteen times more than one of the majority of people. It's a mind-blowing difference. Even the most brilliant genius cannot be sixteen times smarter than everyone else. How is this possible?

I think the answer lies in the false assumption that intelligence alone creates insight and value. I believe wealth and well-being are created when a missing link—I'll call it the "wealth creation multiple"—is factored in with a person's intelligence and effort. That missing link is the Idea.

I believe ideas are the most valuable things in the universe. But while ideas are the ultimate source of value, only individuals and small teams can create, appropriate, develop, and clothe ideas in business reality. An individual's power derives from the strength and success of his or her ideas. But we are only beginning to understand how important ideas are, how to choose between powerful and trivial ideas, how to combine and leverage ideas, and how an idea's potential can best be liberated and renewed.

As we saw in chapter 1, the 80/20 principle tells us that a few ideas are much more powerful than others. Albert Einstein was able to create the theories of relativity not just because he was a genius, but also because he was playing around with powerful ideas from early quantum physics. He knew which ideas to select and examine as well as how to give those ideas a unique twist.

Human creation, while relying on individualistic inspiration, always follows the same pattern. The pattern can be described using the 80/20 principle to look beyond the "average" nature of reality and isolate the most powerful forces and ideas behind success—to focus on the "vital few" rather than the "trivial many."

Creativity itself cannot be reduced to a cookbook formula. Individual insight and knowledge will always be essential. Yet anyone who has deep knowledge or great instincts about a particular area or endeavor can speed up the process of creation, and be more confident of achieving a positive result, by using the 80/20 principle. Understanding the principle enables individuals to create more, in less time and with fewer blind alleys. It is my hope that, once the power of the 80/20 principle to help individuals create is understood, many more people will step forward to try their hand at creating something new and valuable. The world can never have too many 80/20 individuals.

Because my own experience of creation has been in business, most of my case studies are about business creators. While you can use this book to help you create a new business venture, the 80/20 principle applies to all fields of endeavor. The ideas and approaches here are relevant to 80/20 individuals from all walks of life.

Individuals versus Corporations

Individuals are the creators of wealth and well-being, and have been for some time. But if we were to ask "What drives the economy and its growth?" or "What creates well-being?" most people would reply "large companies," "the stock exchange," "capital," "government," maybe even "not-for-profits." Very few would reply "creative individuals."

If we turn the question around and ask where wealth accumulates, most observers would point to the still-dazzling market valuations of the largest corporations (those that haven't been sunk by the unethical behavior of their CEO, that is). In each market, value is concentrated in a few select stocks. In each industry, two or three megacorporations control a majority of the market. Big business appears to be where value resides.

In a global economy where the big get bigger and wealth goes to the biggest, what place is there for the individual? Capital and corporations appear to rule the roost. Individuals have to fit in with powerful organizations as best they can, both in their working lives and as citizens.

Or do they? Is there another way of interpreting what is happening?

Individuals: The Magic, Invisible Force behind Growth

A final and very important link between the 80/20 principle and creative individuals is the recent and probably unstoppable trend that favors individuals over capital, and creative people over organizations. At first, this assertion may seem strange, but I believe that we live in a world that increasingly favors individuals over collective entities. Here's why:

Consider how the economy grows. Does it grow because big companies march ever forward, or because small companies grow from nothing into big companies? Research by Hewlett-Packard and the Corporate Strategy Board shows that as companies enter the *Fortune* 50—the fifty largest U.S. corporations—their growth slows down from a range of 9–29 percent a year to 3–4 percent. Ninety-one percent of companies that became big enough to enter the *Fortune* 50 then slowed down and never grew substantially again without acquisitions.[2] Mergers and acquisitions are evidence of the inability of big business to grow, not the reverse; gigantic companies have to grow their earnings through acquisitions because they cannot grow themselves.

The economy grows because small companies grow. Behind every small company success story is an individual or small group of individuals. Individuals are at the heart of small company growth. But it's also true today that individuals are often at the heart of big company growth.

Take Microsoft, a company that did not exist thirty years ago. Twenty years ago it was worth almost nothing; today, $286 billion. Is Microsoft evidence of corporate hegemony, or of individual enterprise; testimony to the importance of capital and corporations, or of individuals?

Microsoft looks like a megacorporation. It is quoted on the stock exchange and was, for some time, the most valuable company in the world. But it is not a typical large twentieth-century corporation. At Microsoft there is no separation of ownership from control, the hallmark of managerial capitalism. The chairman, Bill Gates, owns 12.3 percent; other directors own 5 percent, and employees in total more than a third. Microsoft has been made by a few very creative individuals and runs largely for their benefit. Microsoft is listed on the stock exchange not because of a *need* for capital; the wealth generated by going public was merely a bonus for Gates and the other owners.

Warren Buffett's global net worth is second only to Bill Gates's. Buffett runs America's largest and most successful conglomerate, Berkshire Hathaway, based in Omaha, of all places. Buffett has a tiny office, employs just a handful of people, and claims to do very little: "Our investment philosophy," he says, "borders on lethargy." How can one individual, supported by a team of trifling size, generate such a fortune? What on earth is going on?

Without most people realizing it, the way in which wealth is generated has changed fundamentally over the past fifty years, and at an accelerating rate over the past two decades. Capital and corporations used to be collective instruments, where the system created wealth and the individual executives were interchangeable and therefore dispensable. Now capital and corporations are instruments, available to individuals and used by them for their own purposes. The corporate systems and the capital are the interchangeable parts; the unique and indispensable element is the individual wealth creator and small teams of creative people. Bill Gates and his close associates are the wealth creators; Microsoft is just the vehicle. Without Warren Buffett, Berkshire Hathaway would have remained a struggling textile company. It is no longer the corporate machine that drives new wealth; it is the creative individual.

Individualism and the Small Team

A creative individual needs a small team, even if the team consists of just two or three people. In 2001 the consulting firm Accenture published a major survey on entrepreneurship, based on nearly a thousand executives. The study concluded that the popular image of the solitary entrepreneur is a myth: "True entrepreneurship is not a lone pursuit but highly collaborative behavior of critical importance to every nation and organization, whatever its size."

The Accenture findings are consistent with the experiences of the 80/20 individuals featured in this book. These 80/20 individuals function within their own space, but never suffer from solitary confinement; they rely on a small team of partners or supporters. 80/20 individuals concentrate on their distinctive strengths and acknowledge their many weaknesses. The weaknesses of 80/20 individuals require a counterbalance; 80/20 individuals are most effective when they surround themselves with others who are strong in different ways.

Contemporary individualism is not a throwback to the splendid isolation of the rugged and self-reliant nineteenth-century hero, or to Victorian political philosophers such as John Stuart Mill. The new individualism recognizes the way social, economic, and intellectual systems have changed over time; today the self-selected small team that supports every individual has become a vital factor in a global economy.

This philosophy is neither elitist nor zero-sum. Highly idiosyncratic individuals respect, encourage, and nurture individualism in other people. The more different and individualistic we become, the more we call forth and depend on other individuals who have utterly different profiles. This is how ecology and society develop, with ever-increasing specialization and interdependence. The time of individuals who gained power by building armies of subservient clones is ending. Such tactics may appear to work for a time, but history proves that they end up destroying, not creating. True creation requires liberation of the human spirit and the rampant proliferation of every individual's unique potential.

The New Society of Cooperating Individuals

It may appear that wealth and well-being come from large organizations, which, however liberal or individualized they claim to be, are inevitably hierarchies.

That thinking is out of date. Progress today comes from the individual and his or her very small team, linked to other teams of similar composition and complementary skills. Where these other teams sit— whether they are part of the same organization, a different organization, or outside any organization—is becoming irrelevant.

There is an ever-shifting, kaleidoscopic network of individuals and their small teams relating to other individuals and small teams. The units cooperate not because they are told to, nor because they are altruistic, but because they benefit from doing so. Cooperating individuals get rich.

Before I go on, I must insert a note about my terminology. From now on, when I write "individuals," I will mean "individuals and their small teams."

Not Fleas versus Elephants

Business guru Charles Handy has recently written about a world of "fleas and elephants."[3] The "elephants" are large organizations. The "fleas" are what he calls "independents," one-person bands such as writers, consultants, or artists. He recognizes that the number of independents is increasing, as people like him leave organizations to become independent businesses.

Yet if all the "fleas" left their organizations to become contractors to their former employers, or to sell their labor elsewhere, business and society would not change very much. Individualism would remain confined to the margins of the economy.

80/20 individuals are not "fleas." 80/20 individuals are not one-person bands. 80/20 individuals cooperate with each other, and with both "fleas" and "elephants," to create substantial, superproductive new business or social enterprises.

80/20 individuals help push the stream of progress forward. They leave behind products or organizations that last, or that lead to even better products and enterprises created by other 80/20 individuals.

80/20 individuals are not lonely independents. They collaborate with many other individuals to create new organizations. These organizations are not "elephants." They are a new species—call them "jaguars" if you wish, or anything else that is fast and sleek.

But animal analogies are misleading because each animal is so similar to other members of its species. On the other hand, each person is unique, as are the organizations they create. The new 80/20 organizations reflect the personality of the individuals that created them. The organization serves the individual, not the other way around.

A New Phenomenon: The 80/20 Billionaire

The 80/20 principle has created a totally new phenomenon: the 80/20 billionaire. The leaders of megabillion-dollar corporations like Black Entertainment Television[4] or Oracle or Goldman Sachs are billionaire owners as well as executives.

It may seem preposterous, but you can do what Bill Gates and many other billionaires have done (although probably on a more modest scale). You don't need to be a technology genius, but you do need to use the 80/20 principle creatively.

Why Is the Rise of Individuals So Exciting?

Why am I so excited by this new perspective on the significance of the rise of individuals? Partly because it allows us to make sense of fresh evidence that has yet to fit into our existing categories and ways of thinking.

For example, there has been much talk in the past few years about how intellectual capital[5] is increasingly more important than financial capital. The concept that knowledge is more valuable than assets is intuitive and useful, yet "real" capital is still the focus of CEOs and financial markets.

This makes sense if you recognize that intellectual capital belongs to individuals, not to corporations. Intellectual capital can only be created by individuals. Apart from patents, brands, and other legally recognized intellectual property (which have always been important), intellectual capital is only valuable if renewed by individuals every month or week or day.

The increased importance of intellectual capital helps explain why individuals are becoming more powerful and corporate systems less powerful. To try to make intellectual capital a corporate asset, or to count it as one, is fitting new wine into old bottles. Valuable intellectual capital quickly becomes real capital held by individuals. The intellectual capital created by Bill Gates, for example, can be approximated by the value of his personal holding of Microsoft stock.

Never before have so many individuals made a personal difference to the world. Yet I believe that for every individual who creates significant wealth and well-being for other people, there are perhaps 10, 20, or 100 individuals who could do so.

One of my main purposes in writing this book is to persuade a large number of individuals to try their hand at creating something big. Very few do this, although most people could if they really wanted to. (I describe how to do it in part two.) It boils down to finding the few things that you are exceptionally good at, finding an idea that fits with your talents and works unusually well, finding other people who can work with you to develop that idea and make it valuable to customers, and using other businesses to do all the hard work for you.

Just fifty years ago most individuals would have found it difficult or impossible to create a new business. Capital was not available. Management was not available. Technology was not available. Ideas were not available. These essential ingredients had all been monopolized by large corporations, or so it seemed. Most people do not realize that today these barriers are gone. They think creating a business is risky. They are wrong. The barriers are self-imposed, mental maps of a bygone era.

If you want to create something new and valuable, you probably can. All you need are the right ideas, the right people, and reasonable determination and intelligence.

Unfortunately, many people who have created valuable new businesses have not been rewarded for their efforts. This book offers many examples of executives and other creative individuals who have made a real difference—sometimes measured in tens or even hundreds of millions of dollars—who have received almost nothing in return. Sometimes, for social or philanthropic reasons, these productive creators have deliberately and happily given and not received. However, many unrewarded creators have been managers at for-profit corporations who watched the benefit of their actions go directly into the hands of passive investors.

This happens because many creators fail to realize all the ways they have created value. They imagine that the corporation is the basic source of wealth, and that it is fair that they receive no more than a good salary. I hope to persuade these people—you may be one of them—to use their power to take a fair portion of what they create.

If there is too great a gap between those who create value and those who take it, the economy will become distorted and growth will slow. If creative individuals are properly rewarded, they will create more, because they have both the incentive and the capital. And this will encourage other creators to put their best foot forward.

Favoring Individuals, Not Big Business

During the twentieth century, the 80/20 principle was mainly visible in large corporations that reinforced their monopoly or semimonopoly status in selected markets. Fewer than 20 percent of the firms in any market ended up with more than 80 percent market share. Typically, each global market ended up with two or three dominant U.S. producers and one or two from other countries. The mainstream automobile market, for example, was dominated by Ford, General Motors, and Chrysler, with Toyota as the main non-U.S. competitor. It was universally imagined that the 80/20 principle would favor corporate size and concentration.

I was not immune from this assumption. When I published *The 80/20 Principle* in 1997, the book applied the 80/20 principle to work, and to individuals, but not to individuals at work. The work section assumed that corporate executives would apply the principle for the benefit of their firms. I broke new ground by applying the 80/20 principle to individuals, but this was to encourage personal effectiveness and happiness, not to suggest starting or developing an individual-centered enterprise.

The 80/20 Individual introduces a different world. Here, individuals can turn an existing market upside down by focusing on one small part of it—the most profitable part. Instead of searching for one firm monopolizing the market, look for the most profitable 20 percent of the market, the part that yields 80 percent of the profit. Find the most profitable 20 percent (or 5 percent, or 1 percent) of customers, suppliers, employees, geographic regions, products, and activities and cut out the rest. If all your profit can be made by branding, why bother to manufacture, distribute, or sell?

In this new world, one market could explode into hundreds. Still, the majority of profit is made in just a few, maybe only one or two, of these niches.

Intel and Microsoft between them can make the majority of profit in a market, yet leave all the donkey work between chip manufacture and software production—the vast majority of physical activity and investment in the PC market—to other firms.

New players don't need to be in every product or every activity; by selecting the best playgrounds, less activity will lead to greater profits. This turns the 80/20 principle against the old monopolists and corporations, and in favor of individuals who start new businesses.

The 80/20 principle essentially takes a large arena—an average—and finds the best seats in the house. It looks for the smallest possible slivers of greatest possible value. In business, that sliver of value is the imaginative individual, who, in exchange, learns to capture the greatest return value, usually through a corporation that he or she owns.[6]

Change Is at Hand

A "tipping point," as Malcolm Gladwell calls it, occurs when a new product, trend, or behavior "tips over" from being confined to a small subculture or area to becoming a mass phenomenon. The tipping point is an invisible line that, once crossed, changes everything, maybe forever.[7]

A disease, like the plague or AIDS, becomes an epidemic. Democracy crosses global borders. Premarital sex or use of the drug Ecstasy becomes a normal activity among teenagers. The mobile phone becomes ubiquitous.

Is the rise of the individual near a tipping point? I think it is. In part three, I'll look at previous economic transformations of the Western world: from feudalism to the early industrial world of small owner-producers and free markets; to the twentieth century's large hierarchical corporations financed by stock exchanges.

A growing number of trends over the last twenty years—especially the detachment of value from assets and ownership, the growth of outsourcing and alliances, the reemergence of owner-managers, and the creation of new economic systems that transcend the boundaries of individual enterprises—all give power and wealth to creative individuals, and indicate the potential for a quite different economic system. The individual-centered world is emerging; in fact, the world has already changed fundamentally. It's time we sat up and noticed.

Navigating the Rest of the Book

Part two, "The Nine Essentials of 80/20 Success," shows how you can create something new and valuable. Each chapter is devoted to one of the nine essentials and is filled with stories of 80/20 individuals, creative individualists who always team up with other people to complement their unique strengths.

Part three, "The 80/20 Revolution," shifts gear to show the consequences of such actions at the level of corporations and the economy.

PART TWO

The Nine Essentials
of 80/20 Success

CHAPTER 3

Use Your Most Creative 20 Percent

This above all: to thine own self be true,
And it must follow as the night the day,
Thou canst not then be false to any man.
—*William Shakespeare,* Hamlet

To thine own self be true—but which self should you be true to? The self that spends a huge amount of time and sweat getting nowhere? The self that engages in destructive patterns of behavior? The self that follows the crowd (all of us, saints and lunatics only excepted, spend much or most of our time conforming to the dictates of others)? Our automatic self? The self that achieves nothing out of the ordinary? The self that could just as well not be a self at all?

No. The self to which we must be true is our distinctive and productive self, our unique self, our imaginative, positive, and creative self, the 20 percent or less of ourselves that contributes more than 80 percent of our impact and happiness.

First we have to find this self, to become aware of the powerful vital few characteristics within ourselves. Then we have to nurture and grow this 20 percent. Only then can we use it to make the world and ourselves richer.

The 20 Percent Spike

What makes a CEO, leader, or manager great is what psychologists call the "spike," and I call the "20 percent spike." The spike is a distinctive strength in a person that is unusually powerful, so it's in your best interest to train and develop your spike to Olympian standards.

Do corporate psychologists, who determine whether you or another short-listed candidate will get the top job, look for well-rounded team players or for oddballs? Intriguingly, the latter. The psychologist wants unusual characters who have a few fantastic strengths. If you have these, the corporation couldn't care less about a long laundry list of things you can't do well or even do at all.

Gurnek Bains, head of YSC, a leading firm of business psychologists, explains: "Any significant leader is not well-rounded. They're all quite different, slightly idiosyncratic characters. The best directors have huge spikes and equally large downsides."[1]

Psychoanalyst Michael Maccoby agrees. He highlights today's "superstar" leaders and draws attention to their lopsided traits: "Today's CEOs—superstars such as Bill Gates, Andy Grove, Steve Jobs, Jeff Bezos, and Jack Welch—hire their own publicists, write books, grant spontaneous interviews, and actively promote their personal philosophies . . . [they] closely resemble the personality type that Sigmund Freud dubbed narcissistic."[2]

Maccoby says that such "productive narcissists" have tremendous vision and self-belief yet are anything but team players. Most would not score well on emotional intelligence or the ability to listen to other people.

Not all 80/20 individuals are "productive narcissists," but many of the new superstars are effective precisely because they are unbalanced. To compensate for their weaknesses, these creative individuals have entrusted their business to other people who are skilled in those areas.

Outsource Your 80 Percent

One of the most important recent trends in business is outsourcing. Companies that outsource get other companies to take on activities they do poorly or that give a much lower return on capital. Ideally, firms outsource the "trivial many" 80 percent of tasks and put all their energy into their "vital few" 20 percent of undertakings.

People can do precisely the same thing, using the same concept as corporate outsourcing. Find the 20 percent (or less) that you are outstandingly good at, then ask other people to perform the rest.

On one level—time—the rich and famous have always done this. You don't catch Madonna standing in line at the supermarket or passport office. Heads of state tend to spend less time fuming in traffic jams than the rest of us. Celebrities pack several lives into one; they live more intensely, devoid of the banalities that bog us down.

We can all export large chunks of ourselves. If you're not good at something, don't do it. Find someone else to do it, or forget about it altogether. Why work hard to become mediocre at something? There are better uses of your time, your energy, your essential self.

Individuals Have Very Different 20 Percent Spikes

This is a vital, but often neglected, truth. Of all the billions of people on earth, only identical twins have the same genetic material. And even identical twins have different experiences, inclinations, partners, and emotions.

Yet we spend most of our lives denying our individuality, trying to pretend that we are just like everyone else. Isn't that weird?

Creative individuals are different. They embrace their individuality more than others do. They are aware of it. They give it more headroom. They cultivate it. They know where it can be used most effectively.

Creative individuals have less need to fit in. They make fewer concessions to "reality," a reality defined by other people.

George Bernard Shaw knew this: "The reasonable man adapts himself to the world. The unreasonable one persists in trying to adapt the world to himself. Therefore all progress depends on the unreasonable man." Now, replace "unreasonable" with "creative."

If you want to create, you first have to find and nurture your 20 percent spike. If you want to create a new business, don't start by thinking about the business. Start by thinking about yourself. What follows are examples of four people who successfully used this 20 percent spike.

Rachel: An 80/20 Management Case Study

For eight years Rachel has managed a branded womenswear business. She has completely remodeled it, taking a near-defunct company and turning it into a small gold mine. Under her tenure, sales have doubled, yet profits have multiplied fifteen times. Her return on capital is 50–60 percent, and she hasn't required any new capital; all her expansion capital has been generated internally. She has provided her parent company with copious dividends.

Rachel inherited one venerable but near-dead brand, which she has revived and rejuvenated. She has also launched two successful brands from scratch.

For a real-world, low-tech affair, Rachel's concern uses little capital. Unlike other garment suppliers in the same group, her division outsources all manufacturing. "Why should I want to manufacture," she asks, "when that's such a low-return activity?" Her division's core competencies are design and selling, but it has little capital tied up in either, as the clothes are retailed through department store concessions. Rachel pays a rent based on turnover, profits, and space occupied, but effectively uses the department stores' capital. She has hired a high-powered design director, yet most of the design work is outsourced.

Rachel fascinates me for reasons I'll explain throughout the book. But first, how did she get started?

"I left school as soon as I could," Rachel explains. "I was no good at anything except math. I suppose I was bored. I couldn't see how my subjects were relevant to what I was going to do.

"One thing I always loved was clothes. I couldn't afford to buy many good clothes, so I decided to sell them instead. My first job was working in a very large department store in Miami. I loved the atmosphere, it was like a huge family. The merchandise was very varied and there was always something going on. These were all things I had never been exposed to. I started to understand that 'things' could be beautiful. That style and taste were qualities you could develop.

"As part of my training, I moved from department to department. First cosmetics and perfumery. Then jewelry. Then trendy fashion, lots from Europe, like Mary Quant. Eventually I made it to the designer room. It was heaven—beautifully made clothes in fantastic fabrics at astronomic prices. Selling to rich women was great fun!

"I wasn't supposed to do it; it wasn't my job, but one day I found myself calculating the profit margin on what we sold. I looked at the invoices and noticed that certain types of merchandise carried fatter margins. It was nearly always the most expensive garments.

"In a way this was natural; people who could afford more wanted the best and didn't care what it cost. But I remember thinking, 'This is really peculiar. These clothes are the best ones to sell, the most expensive, and yet they take little more effort to sell, sometimes less effort, than the cheaper merchandise.' So if our department wants to take more cash, we should put all our sales push into the more expensive stuff. But, you know, it's also true that the percentage margin on the clothes is greatest. So we win both ways. We take more money, but we also make more profit for each dollar we sell. That's when I decided that I should always try hardest to sell the top of our range.

"I noticed another thing. The worst times were when we had to mark down the dresses and suits. And we always had to mark down more than we expected. We were always too optimistic, or rather our directors were. Sometimes I wondered how we could make money at all.

"I decided that if ever I got to be the boss, I would be pessimistic. I would expect to sell less at full price, and more at big markdowns. That way I would make more profit than expected, not less.

"You might say that I was daydreaming. A girl with no credentials would never become the boss. But it's a funny thing. I knew I could do it; I knew that if I became the boss I would be a great boss. It wasn't boasting, I never said anything to anyone else, not even to my best friend. But I knew that I could do it, I knew that I had flair in selecting clothes, and I knew I could do the sums better than anyone else seemed to be able to. I knew it was me. I would be more 'me' if I was the managing director than if I was the salesclerk.

" 'Rachel,' I said to myself, 'you will become the boss.' And I did.

The most difficult part about my current job was getting there. It's been smooth sailing."

Rachel is an excellent example of an 80/20 individual using her creativity to the fullest, yet still working as a manager in an established corporation. Her 20 percent spike is her ability to select merchandise with a very commercial approach—to pick products that will sell very well but at fat margins. This is very unusual in the mainstream market. I will use her and her 80/20 enterprise as an example throughout the book.

Creative People Fit In

Rachel tells me, "It's really odd, but I'm more myself there [at work] than I am at home. I can express myself more. The work, the people, and me . . . they fit together. You say it's difficult to create. I don't agree. When I'm there, I find it the easiest thing in the world."

To create, you must belong. If you work for a firm where you can't be yourself, you may create, but only against the grain. You could create much more someplace else.

Imagine the setting where you could be most fertile. Then create it!

Bjorn-Ingvar: An 80/20 Case Study in Publishing

In the early 1980s, Bjorn-Ingvar was happily employed as a junior professor of English at Göteborg University. He was also a loyal member of his local Lutheran mission church. The church had a tiny, unprofitable business publishing prayer books. Because Bjorn-Ingvar was a professor, the church asked him to look after this enterprise on a part-time, unpaid basis. Bjorn-Ingvar agreed, combining it with his university job.

Bjorn-Ingvar realized that the economics of publishing depended on having a few titles that sold exceptionally well. His prayer books would never fit this bill. So he looked for one or two secular titles that he could take on, although always ones with a wholesome Christian bias. It turned out that Bjorn-Ingvar had an eye for unlikely bestsellers.

The activities of the little publishing house began to demand more time. So, because this was a good cause and something he enjoyed,

Bjorn-Ingvar gave up his professor's salary and accepted a small honorarium from the church to run the publishing house.

Soon the firm's reputation grew among Swedish booksellers: Bjorn-Ingvar's books always sold well. Given his channel into the booksellers, he now looked for successful English brands that he could distribute. Again, because he chose the brands very selectively, this business grew very profitable.

By the start of the 1990s, Bjorn-Ingvar had started to buy up other Swedish publishing houses, but always specialist firms such as those publishing computer manuals. The publishing house was now very much larger than the church that had founded it. Without any capital, without any corporate structure, and initially without any managers, Bjorn-Ingvar had created a business worth tens of millions of U.S. dollars.

And still Bjorn-Ingvar was on pretty much the same honorarium, adjusted for inflation, that he had accepted ten years earlier for supervising the production of a few prayer books. His pay was linked to that of church ministers, well below the average Swedish wage. "I work for the cause and for the church," he admitted. "If I have created a business worth millions, is this more valuable than the work of a pastor who tends to people's souls?"

Today the business Bjorn-Ingvar created—Libris Media AB—is a major Swedish publishing house run by professional managers with large salaries. Bjorn-Ingvar left a few years ago to create another small publishing enterprise, this time on his own account. Yet it is clear he is not motivated mainly by money. He says, "I just love building businesses. I love this one just the same as the church business in its early days. What I really enjoy is doing what I do well, which is finding books and related brands of high standards that will have great popular appeal."

Bjorn-Ingvar had a very precious gift—an instinct for what his specialized audience would buy in droves. As an 80/20 individual, he delighted in putting inspiring, spirited books in front of a large congregation. His greatest reward, as with all 80/20 individuals, was in making a difference.

Olivo: An 80/20 Social Enterprise

Olivo Boscariol is a Frenchman of Italian ancestry who lived in Paris as a self-employed picture restorer. When his first child was born, he and his wife wanted more space so they moved to the small medieval town of Provins. Though they loved living there, there was one drawback: no pictures to restore.

Boscariol eked out a living as a night watchman. But he became fascinated by the medieval floor tiles on display in the town museum. He knew nothing about ceramics, yet after three attempts managed to get a grant from the local government, together with some support from industrial combine Saint Gobain, to set up artisanal production of medieval floor tile replicas. The government grant specified that he should employ only those who, like himself, were on the lowest scale of unemployment benefit.

That was in 1992. Now, Boscariol's business exports tiles to the United States and the United Kingdom and has major contracts for public buildings all over France.

Although his business makes money, this is not Boscariol's main interest. "I love the tiles themselves," he says, "and I knew that this business would reflect what I do best. My main satisfaction today is helping the lowest of the unemployed set themselves and their families on their feet again. I look for those whom everyone else thinks are unemployable, but whom I know can become interested in the tiles. If they like the tiles, I know the people can be salvaged."

Boscariol has an almost religious fervor about helping the desperately unemployed. "Over the past nine years," he tells me, "my business has saved fifty such people." "Saved" is a strong word to use, but it is appropriate. "Typically they stay with me for two or three years, and learn so much that they then go off themselves into the productive economy. Many of them start their own little businesses. My prayer is that they will then do what I am doing, recycling other 'hopeless' people into work that they enjoy and whose products give pleasure to many people."

Perhaps because of the medieval surroundings, Boscariol reminds me of founders of the great monastic orders. They also concentrated on their 20 percent spike, pursuing their passion and saving other people. Today we would classify them as not-for-profit entrepreneurs, but the category is unimportant. What does matter is that—like Boscariol—Benedict, Francis, and Dominic all created something new and valuable, something that reflected their own vision and the essence of their individuality. The essence of being an 80/20 individual is to focus your life around a unique attribute of your personality—one that is of vital importance to you and that can provide what other people need or want in an appealing way.

Jamie: The 80/20 Case Study in Broadcasting

One of the last places where you would expect a young and junior individual to be able to make a huge economic difference is the British Broadcasting Corporation (BBC). The "Beeb" is a monolithic bureaucracy still financed through the government-set license fee funded by anyone who watches a television in the United Kingdom. But the power of 80/20 individuals can reach even into the Beeb's deep recesses.

When thirty-year-old Jamie Reeve, a friend and former business partner, joined the BBC in the mid-1990s, I thought he was crazy; I predicted that he would become frustrated and make no impact. But I failed to take into account his 20 percent spike: his unique insight into the connection between broadcasting and the Internet. In the early 1990s he had told me how important the Internet would become to business (I ignored him). When he joined the BBC, his objective—which had nothing to do with his job there—was to get the BBC to post its content online.

"I was probably about number 105 in the BBC management hierarchy," Reeve told me, "but I had an idea, and I knew that John Birt, the director general, was a creative individual, too. What if I could organize a trip for him to go to Silicon Valley and Seattle and meet all the movers and shakers, and get him excited about the prospects?" Reeve not only succeeded in convincing Birt to take the trip but, to his surprise, John Birt insisted that he come along, too.

"I will never forget that trip in July 1997," Reeve continued. "Imagine. Just John Birt, Bill Gates, and me . . . talking for two hours about what the Internet was doing, and how valuable the Beeb's content was. By the time we came back John was completely sold on the idea."

In November 1997, BBC Online was launched. It is now the most successful content site outside the United States, with about 10 million users worldwide and 300 million page impressions a month. If BBC Online were sold today, industry observers estimate it could be worth $1 to $2 billion.

Reeve and Birt have left the BBC. Birt now chairs the Lynx specialist media venture capital fund, backed by Virgin and Bear Stearns, where Reeve is a partner.

How to Tap into Your Most Creative 20 Percent

1 Identify Your 20 Percent Spike

While psychologists stress that complete self-awareness is rare, there are various techniques for improving it.[3] Identifying your 20 percent spike is a great deal easier, so it's a good starting point. You may not be aware of all your defects and downsides, but chances are that you know what you enjoy doing.

You may find it helpful to use a firm of vocational or business psychologists to help you, but below are some questions that should help you zero in on where your creative energies lie.

Ask yourself the following questions and record your answers. Then ask about a dozen people who know you well and whom you trust (your life partner, close friends, business partner, your boss, some peers, or even a few people who work for you) to answer the questions. Be sure to demand accurate, honest feedback.

The 20 Percent Spike Questionnaire

Question	Your Answer
❖ What sort of thing really excites [name]? What have you heard [him/her] be most passionate about? [Do not confine this to work-related matters.]	

Question	*Your Answer*

❖ Imagine that [name] becomes
famous in [his/her] lifetime.
What possible things might
[he/she] become celebrated for?

❖ What is the single most
distinctive thing about [name],
that defines [his/her] individuality?
What is most difficult and
idiosyncratic about [him/her]?

❖ What do you think [name]
would be happiest and most
fulfilled doing?

❖ What one thing is [name]
best at, and better at than anyone else you know?

❖ What occupation or role
do you think [name] is best
suited to?

❖ Think imaginatively about a
different arena or activity that
[name] might be excellent at,
preferably far removed from
[his/her] current job. Be creative
and surprising, perhaps not
entirely serious.

❖ If [name] were to start a new
venture that becomes extraordinarily
successful, what might that new
enterprise be? Use your imagination.

2 *How to Work on* Your *20 Percent Spike*

Once you've decided what your 20 percent spike is, you have to train, develop, and hone it. Imagine, for example, that your 20 percent spike is thinking the unthinkable. You excel at coming up with radical new ideas that could transform an industry. Many of the ideas may turn out to be nonsense, or infeasible, but you need only one success to make a fortune.

How do you train and develop such an unusual skill? Like an athlete in training, the key to stretching any skill further is to *use it repeatedly.* You need to find situations where you can exercise your spike. Clearly, the scope to do this is limited in most companies. So if this is your spike, you need to find a consulting firm that specializes in strategic innovation. Get a job there, work for many different industries and clients, and test yourself against the best colleagues in the firm.

As with any skill, daily practice is most important. Become obsessed with your spike. Read everything relevant. Talk to the experts and observe how they deal with difficulties. Compare notes. Feed your passion. Accentuate your own distinctive approach and cultivate your unique style. But above all, practice. Practice in real life, practice in your imagination. Assign yourself tasks. Imagine there's an Olympic competition in your spike, and what you must do to win the gold medal. Then do it.

Your 20 Percent Spike and Your New Venture

In the next few chapters, I'll show that the nature of business opportunities is greatly misunderstood. The raw materials of business success—powerful ideas and great people—are abundant. But the idea of the 20 percent spike implies that you should not settle for just any old opportunity, however great it may be.

Instead, you must look for the specific opening that you can capitalize on better and more creatively than anyone else. Make no assumption about where the next opportunity might arise. It could involve working within your existing company, teaming up with a competitor, or starting a new venture. Your objective should be to discover the ideal setting where you can best utilize *your 20 percent spike.* Once you identify the right environment in which to cultivate your idea, you can bring it to life.

Remember, most people have little difficulty finding something they do very well. But your destiny as an 80/20 individual is to find a venture inside or outside your organization that is better suited to you than to anybody else, an endeavor that nobody can do as well as you.

What about the 80 Percent of Things You Don't Excel At?

You'll need other people: partners probably, supporters certainly. Your Olympian strength—the 20 percent—requires the 80 percent to be supplied by other people. You need a small team to be effective.

It has taken me some time to realize this. I used to think that the 20 percent was enough to focus on, but I found I still fell short of my full potential. As a perceptive reviewer of *The 80/20 Principle* commented, the meat in a hamburger (the 20 percent) needs the bun (the 80 percent), or it's not a hamburger. This does not invalidate the 80/20 principle. You should still focus on your vital 20 percent, but you should ensure that the remaining 80 percent is supplied by other members of your team.

In any case, it is often difficult to determine someone's 20 percent; both the 20 percent and the 80 percent change over time as one learns and experiences more. We must be aware of the new 20 percent emerging within ourselves, and give it priority and support—from ourselves and from our small team.

There is an emotional need for teams, as well. Human beings need social support. Our 20 percent needs to be protected and encouraged to evolve within robust and hospitable social situations.

Nurture your team: If they are not equal partners with you, think of them as supporters, not as employees. Your success must be their success as well—they must benefit from being part of your world, just as you benefit from them being part of yours.

Do You Need Partners?

You have to decide whether your strength is broad enough to sustain success in your ventures.

Here's the test: If your 20 percent spike is a sufficient basis for a successful new undertaking, you don't need partners. If it isn't, you do. But don't be so quick to assume you can do it alone.

My first venture was a management consultancy specializing in business strategy. My 20 percent spike, I believed, was strategic insight; I could answer questions like "What should this firm really be doing?" Yet I didn't think this was a sufficiently broad basis for a successful firm competing with the likes of McKinsey, Bain & Company, or Boston Consulting. Specifically, I was able to pinpoint two essential skills that I lacked: the ability to do "heavy-duty" quantitative analysis, and the ability to lead and manage a serious professional firm. Without these ingredients, I could have kept myself and a few employees busy, but could never have built a significant and enduring firm. Thankfully, I had two partners who covered the bases I couldn't: Iain Evans, a world-class analyst, and Jim Lawrence, a superb leader.

What should the 20 percent spikes of your partners be? To pose the question is to answer it. Their 20 percent spikes must consist of whatever is necessary for the unique success of the new venture that you cannot provide yourself.

Deciding What to Create

When you have decided on the inimitable power that you and your partner(s) have as individuals, you're ready to move on and decide what you will create together. Chapters 4 to 6 show how the 80/20 principle can guide you to your ideal business domain.

CHAPTER 4

Spawn and Mutate Great Ideas

There is no force on earth so powerful as an idea whose time has come.
—Victor Hugo

E very business can be described in words. In some ways, the idea behind the business is its most fundamental definition. James Champy has expressed this view trenchantly:

> *People like to think that businesses are built of numbers (as in the "bottom line"), or forces (as in "market forces"), or even flesh and blood ("our people"). But this is wrong. Businesses are made of ideas—ideas expressed as words.*

Champy is exaggerating. Enterprises have all these attributes at once: They are numbers, forces, things, people, *and* ideas. Businesses are living, moving entities that we can create and capture using all these things.

Nevertheless, there is great power in viewing businesses as ideas. An idea can be expressed in numbers; in a mathematical formula; in a graph; in a picture; or, with greatest versatility, in words. If numbers are the music, words are the lyrics of business.

For those who like mathematical expressions, we can write:

Any enterprise = Ideas + Numbers
Any enterprise = Lyrics + Music

This chapter is going to concentrate on the ideas behind the business: the words, the lyrics. (I will explain the numbers in chapter 5.) By applying the 80/20 principle, you will look for your unique new idea. This is not as difficult as it sounds. The truth is that in any sphere of business there are just a few powerful ideas. If you latch on to one, two, or three of these and adapt them to your unique abilities and market, you can build a successful new enterprise, inside or outside your current company.

Your quest is to find the vital few ideas that can drive you to success.

Business as Ideas

Every new project, product, or organization must start with an idea. What is your new business idea? And how can the 80/20 principle help you bring it to life?

The progressive, useful, dynamic part of life consists of the tremendously productive, yet few, forces that produce nearly all the results. But the 80/20 principle is dynamic itself; new forces lead to new results. Every productive 20 percent has its own most productive 20 percent. This becomes most apparent over time, as the process repeats.

The computer is a brilliant example of the 80/20 principle at work. Astounding results come from a successful process—such as miniaturization—that is replicated ceaselessly. Computers were once the size of large rooms. Repeated innovations such as the semiconductor and microchip have enabled computers to perform better and cheaper, while taking up a fraction of the space.

The trivial 80 percent may appear to be waste, but if you view the process as infinite, each 80 percent was once necessary. Without the trivial many, the vital few cannot emerge.

Life is an experiment. We are running in a maze, and the 80/20 principle signposts the exit.

Natural Selection and Business Genes

The dynamic 80/20 process of natural selection is an extremely apt way of viewing ideas. Genes that drive the reproductive process of natural selection can be viewed as pure information—in other words, ideas. And essentially all ideas work like genes.

Like plants and animals, humans would be useless machines without the genes that drive us.[1] Similarly, ideas—what I call "business genes"—drive success in business.[2]

Business genes are packets of beneficial economic information, ideas that are useful for business. Just as success in life is influenced by having the best genes[3] and being the best available vehicles for housing these genes, success in business depends on having great business ideas and being the best available vehicle for bringing those ideas to a specific market.

Business genes are useful ideas about which products and services to provide, which customers to serve, and which suppliers to use. These ideas dictate how to deliver your product, how to find and coordinate the right partners and employees; how to make a higher return on capital than anyone thought possible; and about anything else that defines a business and helps it create new wealth.

Which Business Ideas Are the Vital Few?

There are two steps to identifying the "vital few" ideas that can bring you success. First, you need great ideas that have proven themselves. Second, you need ideas that fit your 20 percent spike.

Great ideas always exist in a chain of successful ideas. Successful ideas have many ancestors and many descendants. The best place to look for your new business idea is in the minority of ideas that have already proven themselves to be highly successful—the 20 percent of vital business genes.

Once you've identified these ideas, you can experiment. Tweak the idea until you find the vital one or few ways it can make you most successful. An example of one of the greatest business ideas is self-service:

allowing your customers to do more of the work themselves while also keeping them happy.

But the great ideas will stay with you only if you are the best possible vehicle for them. If you can't take the ideas and make better use of them than anybody else, fortune will desert you. Choose ideas that resonate with your most creative 20 percent, ideas that find their destiny in you.

Competition at the Level of Ideas

The most important competition in business—the winnowing of the trivial many and the triumph of the vital few—takes place at the level of business ideas. In every form of business competition—whether a fight for new products, technologies, or management techniques—only a few winners will survive. And even these winners will be replaced by better versions of themselves.

Real competition, for instance, does not take place between competing firms or their products; rather, it's a battle between *ideas*. For every product that reaches the market alive and well, many ideas were tossed before reaching the drawing board, many died on the drawing board, many were scrapped during the development phase, and many failed in the test market. Only the strongest survived.

Successful Products End Up in a Museum

While the 80/20 principle is essential in bringing good ideas to life, it can also lead to their demise. For every good idea, better versions of the same idea or other ideas that serve a similar purpose arise and kill the original.

An example is one of the most useful ideas of the twentieth century: the Model T Ford. By giving the middle and working classes the freedom to move, it transformed society. As David Hounshell, the historian of mass production, wrote, the Model T "was as much an idea as it was an automobile . . . an unchanging car for the masses."[4]

But where do we find Model Ts today? Not on the road, but in a car museum. And it's not because the Model T failed—it died because it succeeded. This wonderful idea was killed by thousands of new, better ideas, all descendants of the first, all intent on killing their ancestors.

The idea of mass-market automobile transportation found many other vehicles to drive it forward, proving that what matters more than the product, or the firm that produces it, is the idea behind it.

Combine and Tweak Previous Ideas

In addition to building on earlier great ideas, every great business innovation has added a novel twist. The Model T automobile started with the marketing concept: "An unchanging car for the masses," to be sold at a low price. Henry Ford created this low price by building on ideas that had already worked in other products for other people. He took the idea of production scale from Andrew Carnegie, who had proved thirty years earlier that if you increased the size of your steel mills, you could drastically reduce manufacturing costs. When building his gigantic car plant, which opened on New Year's Day, 1910, at Highland Park, Detroit, Ford instituted three more ideas that had proved successful elsewhere: moving lines of work-in-progress; machinery that turned out modular parts; and a schedule to keep production lines flowing smoothly. Everything Henry Ford did had been done before—but in a different context. This doesn't diminish his achievement, but it should demonstrate that your own task is easier than you might have thought.

If you have a great idea, and an objective, you can borrow from other powerful business ideas to see your vision through. Charles Sorensen, who worked with Ford for forty years,[5] should give hope to us all:

> Henry Ford had no ideas on mass production. He wanted to build a lot of autos. He was determined but, like everyone else at that time, he didn't know how. . . . The essential tools and the final assembly line with its many integrated feeders resulted from an organization which was continually experimenting and improvising to get better production.

Tweaking and adapting successful ideas proceeds in many different ways. It starts in your mind. What possible variants of a flourishing idea can you dream up? You'll reject most of these ideas instantly because they're infeasible, unattractive, or both.

Next, you should float the remaining few by trusted judges. Then use the few surviving ideas to make prototypes—in words or models—and test them in front of potential customers. For new products, you may conduct market research, or survey focus groups or a test market. A new business idea may be tested by exposing it to venture capitalists or other fund providers.

The chances of success for your new business, product, or service are dramatically higher if all of the following are true:

❖ The idea is a version of one that has already proved to be successful.

❖ The version you decide to pursue has a very large number of variations and has survived a serious process of business selection, by proving itself superior to the other variations.

❖ The idea, although a variant of another successful idea, is unique—nobody else is pursuing it.

❖ The idea is more economical than the original idea: a better product or service at the same cost, or a similar product or service at a lower cost. Superior economics always translate into higher returns on capital.

❖ The idea complements and takes advantage of the 20 percent spikes of you and your partners—it reflects, and can be reinforced by, your idiosyncrasies.

Mutants in Consulting and the First Business Gene: "Management Consulting"

To anyone interested in management consulting, the name McKinsey is magic. McKinsey & Company is the most venerable consulting firm, and probably the world's most prestigious and successful one. In fact, when describing themselves McKinsey people write "Firm" with a capital F.

Although founded by James O. McKinsey in 1926, McKinsey was put on the map by Marvin Bower in the 1940s. His 80/20 idea was that management consulting could be a profession, just like the law, and that McKinsey should embody the highest professional standards in its dealings with clients.[6]

Today this might seem an odd aspiration; the profession of management consulting is well established. In the 1930s and 1940s, however, management consulting was a fly-by-night and untrusted novelty. In contrast, Bower insisted that McKinsey should put the client's interests ahead of those of the Firm or the individual consultant. Client service, client confidentiality, integrity, and responsiveness in dealing with clients: These values were drummed into the McKinsey cadre.

But where did Bower get these ideas? "All" he did was appropriate a successful model from another profession. Every notion he had, every innovation in language and behavior, came from the law. Before Bower, management consultants "worked for" clients. In contrast, lawyers had "client engagements." After Bower, so too did McKinsey.

It was enough. McKinsey became synonymous with high quality management consulting. The Firm defined its markets as "the board room" and during the 1950s and 1960s had client engagements with most of the world's largest multinational corporations. Each engagement was led by a highly experienced McKinsey officer, typically a man who had seen it all and done it all, whose authority was sealed by gray hair and an impressive collection of hats.

The First Mutation

In 1963, out of total obscurity, a new star was born: The Boston Consulting Group (BCG). And its invention happened pretty much by chance. After being fired from Arthur D. Little, Bruce Doolin Henderson (1915–92) decided to found his own consulting firm, which initially boasted "one man, one desk, and no secretary."

Henderson's 80/20 idea was that BCG should specialize in "strategy," employing smart business school graduates as its analytical engine room. Before this, strategy did not exist as a recognized discipline. Henderson fused two thriving, yet low-margin concepts—market research and financial analysis—together to create strategy.

Previously, market research was solely a tool for marketing departments, while financial analysis served the accounts department. But strategy, the combination of the two, Henderson claimed, should be the concern of top management.

He targeted McKinsey's existing market with his "new" product and delivered it in a new way—replacing gnarled industry veterans with twenty-something business school analysts.

Because they invented it, strategy became whatever Henderson and his colleagues said it was. They were the inventors and propagators of "business genes" long before the term had been invented. They created a loose intellectual monopoly on the province of management ideas, ideas that would rule the world. Bruce's obituary in the *Financial Times* said that "few people have had as much impact on international business in the second half of the twentieth century."

The Second Mutation

In 1970 a group of senior BCG vice presidents led by Bill Bain left BCG to form Bain & Company. Bain added one crucial new aspect to the DNA invented by BCG: the gene of "CEO relationships."

In 1980, I left BCG to join Bain & Company. What amazed me then, and still does, is how a firm could be so similar and yet so different. Same product, same type of employees, same type of client, same type of analysis, same glitzy offices—but a totally different commercial formula based around serving the interests of the chief executive officer, and a dramatically different internal style based on discipline, hierarchy, and teamwork, as opposed to BCG's anarchic, market-based individualism.

Bain also enjoyed different rewards. While BCG's growth and profitability were the envy of most firms, in its first ten years Bain far surpassed BCG in both areas.

The business gene originated by McKinsey found new vehicles for its replication and expansion: first BCG, then Bain, and, ultimately, a host of other new strategy consulting firms. So powerful were the

McKinsey, BCG, and Bain genes that not one of the new firms with these genes failed, a truly remarkable record. The "strategy consulting industry" started by BCG in 1983 has grown at a compound annual growth rate of about 20 percent: a fantastic record.

The Third Mutation

In 1983 two other Bain partners and I split off to found our own firm, initially called the LEK Partnership (later, LEK Consulting). We began as a slightly pale imitation of Bain & Company, but without their reputation, we had to evolve our own differentiation.

It began with a lucky blunder. In our second year of operation, we had plenty of demand but lacked staff, so we went on a hiring binge. We tried to hire twenty MBA graduates from the top U.S. schools such as Harvard Business School and ten twenty-one-year-old graduates from Oxford and Cambridge. This ratio of two consultants to every associate consultant was the daring level that Bain had reached; hiring the junior people added extra leverage to the practice.

MBAs, however, saw us as a risky startup. We made many offers but almost nobody accepted.

On the other hand, either because they were more entrepreneurial or more naïve, we were inundated with excellent undergraduate candidates. They didn't seem to care that we were new and they rated us on the same level as McKinsey, BCG, and Bain—a preposterous idea at the time. We made thirty offers to undergrads. I assured my partners that no more than ten would accept. In fact, twenty-eight did.

Our staff structure was bizarre. Three partners, four consultants, and nearly thirty associate consultants, none of whom, initially, knew anything about business or strategy. What could we do? We had to find something for our young people to do.

And what they did, very well, was computer analysis of our clients' competitors. Our firm's 20 percent spike was heavy-duty competitive analysis, directly reflecting the superb quantitative skills that Iain Evans brought to our partnership. We trained all our people to do competitive analysis, and found it ideally suited to young professionals.

Before long we stumbled across another way of selling the same work in a different and more lucrative market: the M&A (mergers and acquisitions) market. More specifically, the "market for clients who wish to make acquisitions in areas they don't fully understand and who are considering target companies that they would like to know a great deal more about." We invented a new product, which later spawned other M&A products—analysis to help win M&A battles and defend clients under bid attack, and strategy for private equity firms and banks backing bids for companies.

It worked like a dream. We grew our staff, revenues, and profits at 100 percent a year throughout the 1980s, and by the time I left in 1989, we employed over three hundred professional staff members in offices throughout the world and we enjoyed some of the highest margins in consulting.

We were extremely fortunate for the genes we inherited and the people who kept them going. We were continuing—at that time unconsciously—the replication and enhancement of powerful business genes. We were following the 80/20 principle: by taking a very successful formula, experimenting with a number of tweaks, and discarding most of them, we built on the vital few variants and found a receptive market.

New Genes for a Cinderella Market

Now, I'll share a different story, where powerful business genes were imported into a dull market, one written off by most observers. If you are currently working in a flat or failing market, take heart. You can use successful ideas from other markets to invigorate your own.

In the early 1990s, the three-star hotel market in England was in disarray. Many hotels were in the red, and return on sales rarely rose above 10 percent. All the big hotel companies were going upmarket, transforming themselves into glitzy four- and five-star hotels.

I was terribly ignorant when I entered this inauspicious market. I knew nothing about hotels. In fact, I had used some of the capital I'd received from selling my stake in LEK Consulting to buy a hotel at the height of a recent boom, only to watch my hotel's high profits spiral into alarming losses.

Serendipitously, I met three hotel consultants who said they could raise the profits of hotels. They took my hotel in hand and worked their magic, turning my property back into profit. But by that stage the market for hotel consulting was drying up. Interest rates had peaked, good times were coming back, and the big groups were once again sniffing around to buy badly run hotels.

My hotel consultants claimed they knew a formula for raising profits of hotels that was valid in good times as well as bad. So I provided the capital for the purchase of one hotel, and transformed a hotel advisory firm into one that owns and runs hotels. The group, renamed Zoffany Hotels, now has ten hotels, each with a return on sales in the 30–40 percent range, essentially the highest in the market. The growth was staggering; the value of the privately traded shares has increased from £1 to £320 (equivalent to going from $1.50 to $480) in this time.

By testing and adapting a large number of winning ideas from up-market hotel groups and from other industries, we arrived at a unique mix of ideas I'll call the Zoffany formula:

- ❖ Focus on the unfashionable part of the market, namely three-star hotels in the centers of medium-sized provincial towns, where the target market is junior and middle-level executives.
- ❖ The hotels must have a high relative share of their local market; that is, there must not be a larger competitor *of the same type* in the vicinity.
- ❖ Take a rigorous "private equity" approach to *buying* hotels; Zoffany buys only if they are objectively cheap according to industry benchmarks.
- ❖ Build a *flatter* management structure than the industry standard. Zoffany has a very small head office and no regional manager tier. Hotel general managers report directly to one of the two Zoffany partners.

❖ Focus on *bedrooms* rather than other hotel operations such as lounges and dining rooms. Zoffany buys hotels where there is scope to add new bedrooms, because accommodation is by far the most profitable activity in its market.

❖ Utilize *cheap development*. When Zoffany builds new bedrooms it does so at a rate well below the cost for competitors, using local builders supervised by one of the Zoffany directors.

This combination of ideas perfectly matches the skills of Zoffany's two leaders, Niall Caven and Nick Sonley. Caven, who was trained as a financier, always asks, "If I bought this hotel for 100 today, could I sell it in a few years for 200 or 300?" Sonley focuses on development: "If we built more bedrooms, and improved their quality, could I sell enough rooms at a sufficient price to double or triple the money I spend on development?"

Scott: An 80/20 Case Study in Yogurt

Scott Lutz, a vice president of marketing and sales, led the development of a great idea in the mid-1990s. His company, General Mills, licenses Yoplait, the French yogurt brand, in North America, and Lutz came up with the simple yet brilliant idea to freeze the yogurt and put it in a tube. The yogurt could then be eaten anytime and anyplace.

Launched five years ago, Go-Gurt has been an enormous success, especially with kids. Its revenues have exceeded $100 million, helping to drive Yoplait to market leadership over Dannon, which was previously nearly twice as big as Yoplait.

Go-Gurt elegantly combined two earlier winning ideas—the appeal of yogurt as a modern and healthy snack, and the need for "grab & go" packaging, allowing products to provide no-stop refueling for kids on the go.

Could you take two very successful ideas and blend them in a fresh way to create something unique and appealing?

How to Enlist and Mutate Great Ideas

1 Circle Your Wagons

Define the domain where you'll use your great idea. Do this in two steps. First, think of the type of business or new unit you wish to develop. Then, identify the ideas that have previously worked best in that territory.

Complement this by gathering and sorting through some great ideas from other industries. Recall Marvin Bower. None of us would have heard about McKinsey if Marvin had simply taken the best from the consulting industry. Marvin's genius was to think about law firms. What other prosperous industries or firms could you emulate? Think of one whose strategies and ideas could be applied to your market in a way no one has done before.

2 Short-list the Vital Few Ideas

Find complementary ideas that can be combined in novel ways. To qualify, each idea must demonstrate that it is one of the vital few. The firms that embody the idea must be unusually profitable, at least in the area where the idea operates. The idea must demonstrate unusual customer appeal, elegant economy, or both. It must offer more for less. Strike out any ideas that fall below the top 20 percent mark for superproductivity.

Whittle away at your shortlist until you have between three and five vital few ideas.

3 Ferment a Unique Brew

Try combining the ideas until you come up with a unique new business idea that you think will work. In some cases the answer will be obvious. I doubt that Marvin Bower jumped out of his bathtub and ran down the streets of Chicago shouting, "Eureka! Make consulting a profession like the law." But his innovation stemmed from one basic idea.

A unique brew may also result from two ingredients, as when Bruce Henderson mixed market research with financial analysis.

Play with different combinations of ideas. If you have five ideas and mix any two of them, you'll end up with ten possible new combinations. If you combine any three or five ideas, you'll have another ten possible mixes. Only a few may be sensible, but then again, only a few will be obvious. Write out the possible combinations and decide which ones might work.

Make sure to study all six factors that contribute to the uniqueness of an idea.

- ❖ Product
- ❖ Service
- ❖ Time (to design or deliver a product or service)
- ❖ Customer
- ❖ Geography
- ❖ Activity (type and stage of value added; examples include design, research, exploration, manufacturing, selling, distribution, or a combination of these variables)

Arrive at a shortlist of one to three new great ideas that define a venture in an exciting and innovative way, and differentiate it from any existing business.

4 Test, Test, Test

Test your shortlist on as many people as possible (exclude competitors and thieves) by asking them to compare two raw ideas—is Idea A better or worse than Idea B? Ask at least ten qualified observers until a majority vote is clear. Then compare the winning idea to Idea C. Repeat the process until you have run out of ideas—or friends!

5 Confirm the Economics of an 80/20 Enterprise

Work out the numbers for the great idea. Unless the numbers demonstrate very high return on capital and higher margins than in earlier variants of the same idea, your new great idea isn't one.

6 Discover the New 20 Percent within the 20 Percent

If things don't go as well as you expected, you may have either too many or too few ingredients of a great idea. Try adding or subtracting variables until the returns characterize an 80/20 enterprise.

Even if your plan seems foolproof, conduct a large number of experiments to vary your successful formula. A new 20 percent of super-successful forces always exists within or adjacent to the successful enterprise. I will return to this point in chapter 11.

Repeat steps 1–6 until you feel confident about the new great idea. Look for great people and capital to launch it. Then do it.

Josh and Vince: An 80/20 Case Study in Person-to-Person Betting

What do you do if you're tired of being used as a pawn in corporate power struggles, tired of making fortunes for other people, tired of having a boss, and above all, ready to run your own show? Vince Monical and Josh Hannah, two highly ambitious young MBAs, faced these very obstacles in the spring of 1999.

Hannah and Monical were consultants at San Francisco's Bain & Company, the management consulting firm where I used to be a partner. They had great jobs and they were doing what they loved—working on venture capital deals. But they wanted more: to own their own company, and to create something big.

"It was a weird time," Hannah says. "The dot-com bubble was expanding like crazy and capital was insanely cheap. If you had a plausible idea, you could get funded.

"But we realized that you had to have a truly *different* idea, yet one based on previously successful ideas. What was the great success story of modern capitalism? It was the market. And how were people making money now? By using the World Wide Web to create new electronic marketplaces—Amazon.com in selling books online, for example. Monical was obsessed by the idea of marketplaces. We looked with envy at the phenomenal rise and rise of eBay. Where could we find another idea for a new marketplace that was just as powerful?

"We looked across all possible business sectors to identify an electronic marketplace that had not been done and that could be profitable. Vince stressed that the new opportunity had to be 'easily mon-etized'—that we must be able to take a cut, to get money out of the marketplace and into our own company. That was the problem with the Web—you could start a business and make it bigger, and get to very high revenues, but how could you make money out of it?

"After weeks of trying to find a fresh idea, Vince and I were riding a BART train home to Berkeley after work on Thursday. It was crowded and we were standing together. Vince whispered to me, 'I think we've come too late to find a new Internet idea. We've talked to death about marketplaces, but the only ones left on the Web are small niches. The only good idea that's left is sports betting—but the trou-ble with that is, it's illegal.'

"I saw in a flash that betting on the Web could be person-to-person, between two people, so it would be different from traditional sports betting. 'Maybe *that* won't be illegal,' I told Vince. 'Person-to-person betting is by far the best idea you've had. It's a natural for the Web. It's easy to get our cut, because money is changing hands. And it's even better than eBay, because we won't have to ship any goods.'

"When we got to the office the next day and did the research, we found that sure enough, person-to-person was just as illegal as betting on the Web with bookies. Then I thought, hang on, that's just Amer-ica. Maybe it wouldn't be illegal overseas. I'd worked in Russia and Australia, and knew that sometimes you could export ideas from America. It turned out that person-to-person betting was legal in En-gland and many other places.

"Gambling was perfect. You could make a marketplace out of gam-bling, and if you were the first and remained the biggest, everyone would come to your site and not that of a competitor. And you could take a cut. The model was just like a stock exchange. If one person thought that one baseball or football team would win a match, and another thought the other team would win, you could stand in be-tween the two people as the broker or matchmaker and take a small fraction of the winning bet. We cut out the bookie. And unlike book-ies, who took 10 to 15 percent from each bet, we would take 2 percent and still make a good profit. We could do this because it was so much cheaper to operate at high scale on the Internet than to have betting offices and all the other costs of real-world bookmakers.

"We wrote a plan, raised $5 million in a first round from an ex-Bain colleague who now worked for a venture fund, packed our bags, and moved to London—the gambling capital of the world—and started from scratch. We raised a total of $45 million in the first six months, and management still kept nearly half the shares in the new firm, which we called Flutter.com. We launched our site in London in May of 2000 and were the first betting exchange in the world.

"Before long, the business was growing at 20 percent per *month* and was clearly going to be a big winner. We had strong position in the market and by far the wealthiest balance sheet amongst the competitors who sprang up.

"We had one problem, and it was a big one. There was a British competitor, Betfair, which had become the largest betting exchange in the UK horse racing market. This is a big industry, and Betfair had managed to become twice as big as we were . . .

"We knew that the biggest player would win. We had to become the biggest and we were gaining on Betfair. But then we thought—why not merge?"

I saw the issue from the other side. By investing $2.25 million in Betfair early in 2001, I had become the largest nonmanagement shareholder and a director. I, too, believed that the largest business would succeed, but I knew that despite its size, Betfair was chronically short of money. In Flutter, Betfair faced a rich competitor that was determined to replace us as leader. Each month, they were gaining on us. So in December 2001 we merged the two businesses.

Now Hannah and I serve as outside directors in Betfair (the name for the merged Betfair/Flutter operation). The business has revenues running at more than $5 billion a year and is still growing over 10 percent a month. It is already profitable, and Hannah and I think it will be worth billions of dollars before long if we manage to retain our market lead.

Flutter and Betfair were brilliant ideas, executed and merged with great aplomb. Yet the idea is simply a new marketplace, similar to the centuries-old stock exchange.

What successful idea is waiting for you to adapt it to another market?

How to Mutate Ideas as a Manager

It is not necessary to start a new company to create huge value through new ideas. 80/20 individuals can often do so in their own organizations, or by joining another established company more receptive to innovation. Here are some examples of well-known companies where visionary individuals made a huge difference:

Ray Kroc at McDonald's

McDonald's was once a small chain of restaurants run by the McDonald brothers. Kroc's genius was to envision a universal business with a simple menu delivered instantly. Could you develop an idea to simplify or speed up your own business, or a key part of it, in a way that would widen its appeal?

Charles Lazarus at Toys 'R' Us

Toys 'R' Us was a children's furniture store until Charles Lazarus thought it might be profitable to sell toys in his store. The new venture was so successful that he jettisoned the furniture and narrowed the focus to discount toys. Is there a new product working so well in your organization that it could become its exclusive focus?

David Collischon at Filofax

Filofax, the personal organizer company, was founded in 1923. But it was not until the 1980s that it became global leader in its niche. CEO David Collischon, a former Xerox employee, transformed the company with a bright idea of selling Filofaxes through retail outlets. Previously, Filofax had been exclusively a mail order product, mainly sold to army and church users. Could you find a new channel of distribution for some of your firm's products?

Fritz Landmann at International Data Group

In 1986, Fritz Landmann started a business, *Federal Computer Week*, within his current employer International Data Group, founded in 1964 by MIT graduate Pat McGovern. *Federal Computer Week* was launched within two months! It was possible only because Landmann was given two vital resources: money and total autonomy. Can you think of a new venture that you could originate and lead within your firm? Don't say they wouldn't let you. Instead, think of the idea, develop the plan (I'm about to tell you how), and then ask. If the answer is no, take the idea to a competitor, or start up on your own.

Rachel: An 80/20 Case Study of a Manager

How well does Rachel's clothing business stack up against the criteria for an original, successful, well-mutated idea?

* She understood her carefully targeted niche markets and the brands that have become synonymous with these markets.
* She specializes in designs from interesting countries, including Bangladesh, Morocco, and Estonia, using a network of freelancers, often from fashion schools, designing clothes exclusively for her.
* She has expertise in selling these products within department stores, generating very high margin per square foot.
* Rachel has a relentless focus on return on sales and return on capital, broken down into each element of activity. (Rachel's second initial is *M,* and the joke within her business is that it stands for "margin.")
* She takes a merchandising approach and manages the business according to realistic expectations of sale prices, therefore requiring product cost to be low enough to make high net margins. Rachel explains: "While all my competitors assume that they will sell their product at full price—so that write-downs and sell-offs hurt their margins—we assume from the start that we will fail. I manage the business assum-

ing that we will sell only 40 percent of our clothes at full price. Of the rest, we assume 60 percent will be sold at 40 percent off, 33 percent will be sold at clearance prices, and 7 percent will have to be written off. We can usually do better than this, but . . . the product cost has to be low enough to sustain this mix of margins."

Rachel's business thrives on variation and improvement. Each season brings a fresh theme and new clothes from new designers for each brand. Each year is a new crusade to sell more to customers and reduce product costs.

"I'm not talking about overhead reduction." She jabs her finger at me. "There's a limit to that. It's the cost of goods that has to come down. I tell my designers each year that the cost priced for each type of appeal has to be such-and-such, which is always lower than the year before. The designers themselves are involved in cutting the costs; they're not just airy-fairy fashion artistes. It has to do with the fabric that we choose and all kinds of things you couldn't imagine. More for less is what you say. We've been doing it for years."

CHAPTER 5

Find the Vital
Few Profit Sources

He that is everywhere is nowhere.

—*Thomas Fuller (1608–61)*

T he 80/20 principle uses numbers to identify the vital few forces that can bring you success. Just as music arranges sounds in a pleasing sequence and combination, so the numbers tell us when we have arranged business in a profitable sequence and combination.

Few businesses are extremely profitable as a whole, yet many parts of businesses are. Using the 80/20 principle, we can identify the most profitable parts of businesses and use them as building blocks for our new opportunity within or outside an established organization.

Using the 80/20 principle to increase your profitability does not require you to start a new business. The same result can often be achieved when managers remodel an existing business to improve the use of capital. As I will explain, the remodeling is not just a matter of vague "improvement" or "cost-cutting"; it involves a radical look at all parts of the business.

Your objective should be to arrive at a *dramatically more attractive and profitable business.* This remodeling usually involves changing both the *customer base*—by targeting a smaller, but more attractive segment of customers—and the *business formula*—by improving the way the new customer is served.

Let me assure managers that almost every existing business can be remodeled to become more profitable. It just requires imagination—and an approach based on the 80/20 principle to identify ways to get very high returns from the capital and other resources used. If you are a manager, as you read this chapter, think about how *you* could remodel *your* business, to double or triple its profitability.

When 80/20 individuals target the most profitable markets, discover the most attractive way of serving customers, and witness their cash flow eclipsing investment—then they'll know that they are managing an 80/20 business.

In chapter 4, you learned to whittle down to the one or two ideas that will help define your new venture. In this chapter, you will begin to study the numbers from profitable fragments of businesses to decide what your new ventures should do. You will use inductive reasoning: By identifying the numerical value of the vital few profitable forces, you will have the ingredients for a successful new enterprise. These numerical details will help you shape your new or improved business from the bottom up.

Finding the Vital Few Profit Sources

Examine the accounts of any company and you will learn that it earns a certain return—for example, 15 percent return on capital. But this is not the whole truth, at least not the interesting truth. Because while a few small parts of the business may earn 60 or 70 percent return on capital, other substantial divisions probably lose money.

In a good year the U.S. economy will grow 3 percent. Yet a few firms will grow at 20, 50, or even 100 percent. In a corporation growing at 20 percent, certain products may double or triple their annual sales.

Look around a large office. Everyone may seem to be busy and productive, but a few people will be adding 10 or 20 times more value than the rest.

Reflect on how you spend your time. A few of your initiatives, based on the amount of time you spend, will create 10 to 20 times more wealth than anything else you do. And several things you do probably destroy wealth.

If you think about the "raw materials" for a new or improved business—the product or service you provide, the customers you serve, the geographic limits of your business, the ideas, technologies, and business models you use, the people you employ, the partners or suppliers you work with—you should focus on two critical issues:

❖ What is going to create the most wealth for the least effort and capital? *This is the wealth-creating question.*
❖ Which raw materials are most crucial to my success? For each type of force (product and service, customer, etc.), which produces 80 percent of the result for 20 percent of the resource? Which are the vital few? *This is the 80/20 question.*

The rest of this chapter gives you the tools to answer these two questions.

I have asked both of these questions several times throughout my career. As the co-owner of a consulting firm, I have identified the vital few profit sources that made my company successful.

Originally, my partners felt that large projects were the vital few, and that we should concentrate our efforts on our largest clients. This would be the right thing to do if 80 percent of our profits came from large projects that constituted only 20 percent of sales revenues.

But when I did the analysis, this proved to be only half right. Large projects accounted for 21 percent of revenues but a whopping 56 percent of profits. Return on sales for large projects was 46 percent, while small projects returned less than 10 percent. The large projects were more than four times as profitable.

But a 56/21 relationship was not enough. To arrive at an 80/20 relationship would require us to delve beyond the issue of large versus small clients. So I asked, "What other types of work will create the most wealth for the least effort and capital?" One answer was "old" clients: clients we had served for more than two years. Analysis revealed an 80/20 relationship. Old clients comprised 26 percent of revenues but a stunning 84 percent of profits. Their return on sales was 55 percent, compared to clients of six months to two years, whose return on sales was 13 percent, and new clients who led to a loss of 31 percent. Old clients were the vital few.

We realized new clients take a lot of work to land. You have to spend a lot of time building credibility through service and results. All new clients are skeptical and price sensitive. Older clients, however, trust you, and you already know how to please them and get results. There's no uphill battle.

Concentrating on old clients might seem a recipe for stagnation: no new clients, no new profits. But this is conventional thinking. 80/20 thinking finds creative ways to increase the most profitable business. So we decided to let the best people in the firm—instead of chasing new business—work to generate more from old clients and make all clients "old" clients. Our goal was redefined: Keep existing clients and raise our billings on them.

We had found our vital few profit sources: existing clients and improved, long-term service. The vital few became the vital many—our existing clients responded to our efforts and gave us more of their consulting business. We were highly profitable and doubled in size each year for six years.

The wealth-creating question and 80/20 question again offered a solution when Robin Field and I rescued an almost bankrupt Filofax in 1990. Robin describes the situation best[1]:

> While Filofax design and features had remained static, the product line width had expanded beyond all control. The same basic binder was available in a bewildering variety of sizes and a huge assortment of—mainly exotic—skins. Name a creature and Filofax would have ordered several thousand binders made of its hide and proudly placed them in its catalog and in stock. I don't know what a Karung is, but I inherited an awful lot of its skin in 1990.
>
> Similarly, name a subject: bridge, chess, photography, bird watching, wind surfing, and Filofax would have commissioned several specialist inserts, had tens of thousands of them printed, and put them in inventory. . . .
>
> The result was, of course, not only a huge overhang of worth-

less stock, not only an administrative burden of vast complexity,
but total confusion among our retailers.

We decided to concentrate on the vital few: the 20 percent of popular products and the 20 percent of customers who gave us 80 percent of our margin. Within three years Field had turned a large loss into a 15 percent net profit. Our volume sales quadrupled, and the stock price jumped.

Making the Vital Few Profit Forces Work for You

Consider three main categories of your business when identifying the vital few profit forces, the 20 percent that gives you 80 percent of profits: people (employees and partners), customers, and products and services.

Who Are the Vital Few People?

Identify the superproductive and supercheap employees and what they have in common.

In my consulting organization, this was easy. The people at the bottom of the professional hierarchy were not just the cheapest to employ; they were also the most productive.

Our professional staff was split into three broad categories. At the top was us—the partners. Next came the consultants, usually around thirty years old, armed with MBAs and attitude. The bottom layer was comprised of associate consultants or researchers. They were younger, around twenty-one to twenty-five, with good undergraduate degrees, and spent most of the day manipulating data and conducting analysis on their PCs.

The partners were expensive; but, after all, we sold the work and usually came up with the dramatic insights. Less gratifying was the cost of the consultants. Their salaries began at $100,000, and many cost much more. The "kids" were a bargain. They had endless energy and often put in eighty to ninety hours a week. Hour for hour, the associate consultants were cheaper than the secretaries.

Consultants, like lawyers, aim to bill all the hours spent on client engagements. The associate consultants were extremely profitable for two reasons. First, we could bill them out at a higher multiple of salary (based on a standard eight-hour day) than we could other staff—a clear clue that they generated more wealth relative to their cost. And two, they worked more hours. The kids were our vital few.

Most consulting firms bulge in the middle: a few partners at the top, a mass of mid-level consultants, and a few junior professionals at the bottom. When we found that the associate consultants were our vital few, we made them the vital many, constructing our industry's first pyramid—one supported by a large number of junior staff at the base. With the kids as our largest group of professionals, our profits soared.

Who Are the Vital Few Customers?

Earlier, I established that in the consulting business the most profitable clients are the old clients. This is often true in other businesses, which is why firms that retain a higher proportion of their clients have much higher profits.

However, in a professional services business owned by its partners, profitability is not the only criterion for selecting clients. The enjoyment and professional satisfaction of the partners and other staff are also important: Professional firms compete for the best staff as well as for clients. A firm of accountants in New Zealand I know grades its clients on the following criteria:

* Whether the staff members like the client
* Whether the staff respects the client
* Whether the client respects the staff
* Whether the client doesn't complain about the fees
* Whether the client pays on time
* Whether the client offers opportunities for growth in billings

1 *Define the Vital Few Extra-Profitable Customers*
If you were to start a new venture in any particular area—and you may want to think of several potential areas where you could do this—

what type of customers would you want? By defining the vital few most profitable customers, you are bound to gain some valuable clues about the possible shape of your future venture.

Try to imagine who would be the most profitable customers in the following areas:

❖ Size of revenues the customer provides.

❖ Length of service the customer needs.

❖ Typical purchase quantity per order (customers who receive large deliveries, even infrequent ones, are often much more profitable).

❖ Main product or service bought (some products are much more profitable than others).

❖ Breadth of purchase. Customers who buy only one product are sometimes much more profitable because that product will have a long run; sometimes customers buying a range of products are more profitable because they will pay top dollar for their less important purchases.

❖ Personality of the customer. Smart customers are sometimes best because they demand improvement of your products, keeping you ahead of the competition. Lazy customers can also be an asset because they are not sensitive to price. Banks make a great deal of money from lazy customers, those who keep a great deal of cash on deposit despite low interest rates. One consulting firm I know deliberately targeted "paranoid" clients because they thought large amounts of consulting gave them security.

❖ Rank of the customer. When selling products and services to other corporations, the most profitable customers are usually the most senior in the hierarchy. Chief executives are often the best clients.

❖ Demographic (such as income level) and lifestyle criteria (such as risk-taker versus risk-avoider, or technophile versus technophobe). My experience, however, has shown that "canned" criteria (those measured by advertising and marketing agencies) rarely correlate with the vital few. The vital few usually cut across canned criteria—what makes them vital is not obvious to marketers.

When defining the vital few, keep in mind that suppliers don't explicitly target them. If the vital few were obvious and assiduously courted by most suppliers, they wouldn't remain extra-profitable for long.

2 *Identify Customers Who Have the Highest Ratio of Value to Cost*
The same product or service may have very different value to different customers. Alternatively, small and inexpensive tweaks of the product or service may enable you to sell to upscale customers and command a much higher price.

Strategy consultants Bain & Company did just that. As you learned in chapter 4, Bain was formed in 1970 when Bill Bain, a senior officer at the Boston Consulting Group, resigned to head his own firm. Bain undertook pretty much exactly the same work as BCG—the product was essentially identical—but he exclusively targeted the top person in any corporation; especially new group CEOs. Instead of selling individual products to division heads or other senior managers, Bain sold exclusive relationships that encompassed many projects, all sponsored by the CEO.

A new CEO often made his mark on his group by implementing the Bain consulting program. Bain projects provided information and insight, which enabled the CEO to make radical changes quickly. Most new CEOs working with Bain were able to impress the financial markets, and watch their shares surge.

The delivery of the product—the process of consulting, the analysis of costs, customers, and competitors—remained unaffected; its unit cost did not rise. But margins and growth did, and the service and the offering were transformed.

By identifying the customers who had the highest ratio of value to cost, Bain became one of the world's top consulting firms.

Bain refused to work for the majority of clients that most consulting firms were eager to court: finance directors, marketing directors, even divisional CEOs of huge companies. A growth strategy that eliminates most potential consulting clients might seem bizarre, but its success proves that the vital few profitable forces overwhelm the trivial many.

What Are the Vital Few Products and Services?

Once you've discovered your business's vital few customers, you must identify the vital few products and services that those customers value, and concentrate on becoming an expert supplier of them.

To find the vital few products and services, study the most profitable players in your market. How do they differ from the rest of the pack?

Imitation is not enough, however. Remember, 80/20 individuals must create something new and unique. To encourage your creativity, apply the following seven themes to your 80/20 spike and the business area that you know best. Mix and match them as needed.

1 Think Small

This is classic segmentation, focusing on only one part of an established market.

For example, the U.S. and European motorcycle markets were once dominated by manufacturers such as Harley-Davidson, Norton, and Triumph that targeted the serious rider. In the 1960s, Honda thought small and introduced much smaller motorbikes to the American market, creating an entirely new market and appealing to many people who were new to motorcycling. BMW later created another market with the development of wide, comfortable bikes for broad-bottomed people.

2 Think Big

Resegment and create a bigger market, either by combining more than one existing product or technology, or by inventing a new application for a product or technology. Here are some examples:

❖ Computers were once sold exclusively to a corporate market, to be operated by trained personnel. When Steve Jobs founded Apple Corporation, he "thought big," believing that there could be a mass consumer market for personal computers (PCs). His vision of a computer in every home was a crazy idea in the late 1970s, as computer operators required substantial expertise to understand the binary code. But Jobs made the breakthrough of designing a simple PC that had a feature called the "GUI" (graphical user interface) that allowed people to use a computer without understanding the first thing about how it worked. Without Jobs's idea, the PC market and widespread use of the World Wide Web might never have happened.

❖ Honda does not base its strategy on conventional market classifications such as motorcycles, lawn mowers, cars, or power generation equipment. Instead, it entered *all* these markets with the commitment to create the world's best small engines—its vital few product—for many types of equipment. Honda's vital few service is its unrivaled expertise and precision in creating small engines and multilevel cylinder heads with self-adjusting valves for many different industries.

❖ Bain Capital has become the world's most successful private equity house by enlarging the definition of the market. In addition to evaluating and financing deals, Bain also devises the strategy for its investee companies and supervises their management. For fifteen years Bain Capital has been the most profitable private equity firm in the world, doubling the value of its investments each year.

❖ Home pizza delivery was once a local market. Expansion was constrained by the limit on how far you could take a pizza while keeping it hot. Domino's Pizza created an international business based on "guaranteed delivery within thirty minutes," facilitated by using an insulated envelope to keep the pizza hot, and a network of motivated delivery personnel.

3 Think Upmarket

For every mass market, there is an opportunity to create a niche serving upscale, wealthy customers.

Examples of products that became "upmarket" include Ferraris, Rolexes, American Express charge cards, private banks, and expensive beer brands.

Toyota, a company boasting fantastic engineering skills and low-cost production, broke into the luxury car market in 1989 with the launch of its Lexus brand. Toyota launched its splendid product with expensive, effective advertising; however, it raised the price on the Lexus far above the extra cost incurred. By 1992 the Lexus brand was small compared to Toyota's total sales—only 2 percent—yet constituted about 30 percent of Toyota's profits.[2]

4 Think Mass Market

For every market largely confined to rich consumers, there is an opportunity to create a mass market by making the product or service much simpler, cheaper, and in higher volumes. Examples include the Ford Model T, package holidays, budget airlines, and fast-food restaurant chains.

5 Pursue Value Innovation: Provide More for Less

This is a very fertile category. Provide better value for a new part of a market that you define and create by adding and subtracting.[3]

Addition means offering some better or extra services, particularly when they can be provided at relatively low cost.

Subtraction means dropping parts of the traditional product or service package while still providing excellent value.

The new combination of products and services offers greater value, but only to part of the old market: customers who like the new mix of product offering and price. Change the mix to appeal to a particular group of customers that you define:

❖ Formule 1, a French hotel chain, provides cheap and small but excellent, quiet, and clean hotel rooms with large, comfortable beds. The rooms are modular and mass manufactured, and you won't find lounges, a concierge, room service, or twenty-four-hour reception, but the good sound insulation and low cost suits many business travelers just fine.

❖ Southwest Airlines offers low fares, frequent flights between the cities it serves, ten-minute check-in times, and automated ticketing at the gate. It's fast, reliable, and cheap—and very profitable thanks to its value innovation. Southwest forgoes many of the expensive services provided by traditional airlines. It doesn't land at large airports or schedule long routes, nor will it ticket bags through to other destinations, feed you, or offer a choice of cabins. Its standard fleet of 737s cuts maintenance costs and delays. It encourages direct payment, cutting out commissions to travel agents and reducing accounts receivable. Southwest appeals to a certain type of traveler who appreciates the trade-offs it makes. And there are now European "no frills" imitators of SWA—most notably, Easyjet and Ryanair—that are enjoying their own success.

❖ European furniture retailer Ikea sells stylish goods at low prices by requiring customers—mainly young parents—to do the hard work of choosing, paying for, picking up, delivering, and assembling the furniture. In return, it offers what they need: innovative design and low prices, late hours, in-store child care, great room displays, and instantly available stock.

6 *Use Direct Distribution Channels*

Channels requiring real estate, on-site inventory, and personal service are expensive. Direct channels are cheap, and are often the clue to creating a new 80/20 venture.

Dell Computer Corporation innovated in 1984 by selling personal computers directly to consumers, cutting out the dealer network by using mail-order catalogs and taking orders by fax and phone. The catalog offers greater choice than is available in a typical computer store, but also means great cost savings for Dell because goods move from factories only when there is real end-consumer demand. Lower inventory translates into a 6 percent cost-of-goods advantage for Dell; the problem with having an inventory of computers is particularly acute, given that technology is always advancing and prices are continually falling. Dell offers lower prices, yet enjoys higher profits than traditional suppliers.[4]

7 *Focus on Activities that Have the Highest Ratio of Value to Cost*
Cherry-pick. Find sweet spots. Identify the part of the value chain—from conception in research through to design, development, branding, manufacturing, selling, and physical distribution—that has the highest profitability, and focus exclusively on that.

What are the hints for finding sweet spots? Find activities that have the greatest customer appeal but require the least capital. Product design, branding, and direct selling are often sweet spots. Manufacturing, physical distribution, and retailing through a fixed store network are often sour spots.

LEK Consulting specialized in the type of strategic advice that could be delivered by its low-cost analysts, the associate consultants. While our young analysts were not ideally suited to talking to senior client personnel, they were skilled at delivering data on markets and competitors.

We soon realized that our young analysts were also adept at gathering data on potential acquisitions; before long, we had developed specialist expertise in assessing M&A (mergers and acquisitions) opportunities. Because M&A work was dear to the hearts of chief executives, and because the expenses for completed acquisitions did not have to be charged to the profit-and-loss statement, it was our dream formula: very high prices, low costs, and fabulous margins.

Similarly, Microsoft works only in the most profitable layer in the computer industry—designing the operating system—while Nike focuses on designing and branding its athletic footwear, contracting out capital-intensive and low-return activities like manufacturing and retailing.

Ramash Vangal and Suman Sinha: An 80/20 Case Study of Managers at PepsiCo

Here is a great example of how managers can transform the competitive landscape by focusing on direct proprietary business channels and on the activities that give the most bang for the buck.

Two managers, Ramash Vangal and Suman Sinha, worked for PepsiCo in India in the early 1990s, when the soft drinks industry was dominated by the Chohan brothers' local brands, including Thumb's

Up and Gold Spot. Because of a government ban on majority foreign ownership, neither Coke nor Pepsi was in the market.

When the ban was gradually relaxed, PepsiCo was allowed to come into the market with a minority partner, provided Pepsi also exported substantial quantities of Indian goods. Vangal, an Indian who had worked for Procter & Gamble before moving to PepsiCo, became the new division president. Vangal viewed Pepsi as a great global brand, and through astute marketing managed to establish Pepsi as the premium cola, taking 30 percent market share within three years. By chipping away at the Chohan brothers' local brands, Vangal hoped to overtake them by the end of the decade.

But Pepsi faced another challenge. When the Indian government further loosened its laws on foreign ownership, Coca-Cola moved into the country without conditions. Seeing the writing on the wall, the Chohan brothers put their operation—still with 60 percent market share—up for sale for $100 million.

At roughly the same time, Vangal was succeeded by Suman Sinha. Sinha had worked for many years in Unilever's Indian business. His 20 percent spike was a combination of strategic insight and a deep understanding of business in India.

What was Sinha to do? The obvious move was to buy the 60 percent market share controlled by the Chohan brothers. Together with the 30 percent Pepsi already had, a 90 percent share would make it very difficult for Coke to enter the market. There was, however, the danger of entering a bidding war with Coke, which would lead either to overpaying for the Chohan business or to losing to a higher bid from Coke. Sinha, however, understood the importance of the bottlers in the system. The most effective use of cash, Sinha believed, was not to buy the Chohan brands, which were of little value in themselves, but to invest directly in the capability of the Pepsi bottlers to improve delivery to their customers—by buying modern refrigerated trucks and glass for the bottles.

Instead of spending cash acquiring the Chohan brothers' business, Pepsi bought out its minority Indian partner, as well as a local soft drinks manufacturer called Dukes in Bombay; most importantly, though, it spent tens of millions of dollars establishing the most modern bottling system in the country. As a result, 40 percent of Pepsi's new bottling distribution was company owned. The other 60 percent was independent, but strongly supported by Pepsi. Because the local Indian bottlers had little or no capital, Pepsi provided the capital used for trucks, glass, and other Pepsi-approved uses.

Meanwhile, Coke paid the Chohan brothers handsomely for a 50/50 joint venture. Coke launched, but their bottlers, strapped for cash, were unwilling to invest as heavily as needed. Many of the bottlers defected to the Pepsi system, where it was easier to fund expansion. Coke ended up in third place in market share, with Thumb's Up second and Pepsi number one.

Huge value in India was created for PepsiCo by its two division presidents of the 1990s. Vangal built a new business from scratch through vision and marketing pizzazz. Sinha realized that cash could best be deployed to build and sustain market leadership. Between them they created $100 million of business value, multiplying by ten times or more the cash invested in the business. They focused on where the cash counted—Vangal in building the Pepsi brand, and Sinha on enabling the bottlers to deliver to customers.

Rachel: An 80/20 Case Study of a Manager

Rachel's womenswear business is highly profitable because she concentrates on developing only a vital few aspects of the overall clothing market. Its specialty is product design, merchandising, and concession retailing within department stores. Done well, these divisions generate high returns and growth, and require relatively little capital. The trivial many avoided by Rachel's business include manufacturing, warehousing, and the ownership of retail premises.

Rachel's focus on its vital few specialties leads naturally to a focus on a vital few people, customers, and products. The most valued and highest-paid people in Rachel's team are all directly involved with product design and selection, selling, marketing, and contact with customers. The products have been grouped into three areas, each with its own brand and each targeted at well-defined, specific customer groups, such as "career women aged twenty-five to forty-five" or "women shorter than 5 ft 5 in."

The proof that Rachel has tapped into the vital few profit forces is evident in the numbers. While most businesses in her industry make 0–15 percent return on capital, she makes 50–65 percent. While other companies that overextend themselves have flat or nearly flat profits of 0–5 percent a year, Rachel's profits have soared from $2 million eight years ago to $30 million today.

When creating the shortlist of the vital few ingredients you want to concentrate on, ask this final question: Will your new venture be unusually profitable and able to grow unusually fast? Unless you are confident of this, and know why, you can't be sure that yours will be one of the vital few new enterprises.

Putting Ideas and Numbers Together

Now that you've identified the profitable pieces of your market, you should be able to clearly state the idea behind your new empire.

Using the consulting industry as an example, in this chapter I've identified these superprofitable pieces of the market:

- ❖ "Old" clients for whom the firm had been working for at least two years
- ❖ New chief executives as clients
- ❖ A pyramid staff structure with an abundance of junior consultants, several mid-level consultants, and a few partners
- ❖ An exclusive focus on a new division of product, business strategy

In chapter 4, I identified the following superprofitable ideas:

- ❖ Consulting as professional engagements serving the board of directors
- ❖ The definition of "strategy consulting" as a new product

❖ The idea of strategy consulting as a process of CEO relationships
❖ The use of maximum junior staff leverage
❖ A new division of strategy consulting, focusing on mergers
and acquisitions

If you are thinking of starting a new consulting business, you
should be pleased by the overlap between the top-down and bottom-
up views. Either would have put my own firm on the right track—but
a synthesis of the two views put us in the best position.

The *detailed view* of profitable segments stresses the importance of
selecting clients who have the potential for bringing in long-term
work, and converting existing projects into new projects with the
same client. We would have missed this if we had merely had an idea-
based view.

The *idea-based* view stresses the importance of innovating a new
division of consulting. Like the detailed view, it shows the place to be
is the boardroom, the client you want is a new chief executive, and
the product you sell should be some variant of strategy consulting.
The idea-based view of business demonstrates the need for innovation—in product development, client relationships, and staff structure—to build on and extend the successes of the past.

If you were starting a new consulting business and wanted to
jump-start profitability, you would probably take all the successful
ideas and profitable components from the past and present, but add a
new product line or process. You would need to ask yourself:

❖ Is my idea a direct descendant of current successes with a
unique niche?
❖ Will the market segment I intend to target be unusually
profitable? Can I be sure that the total business will be,
too?

Does Your Potential New Business Perfectly Fit Your 20 Percent Spike?

If you're not the best person to create or remodel a new business, you'd better change the business definition or find a partner who understands your business idea and mission.

Now that the numbers and people are in place, you'll need to consider one more dimension of business before finalizing the market, product, and service of your 80/20 business: time.

CHAPTER 6

Enlist Einstein

For tribal man space was the uncontrollable mystery.
For technological man it is time that occupies the same role.
—*Marshall McLuhan*

In 1916, Einstein argued in his general theory of relativity that time is not independent of space; rather, instead of three dimensions of space, there are four, time being the fourth.

The relativity theory changed our ideas of "space" and "time." According to Einstein, space and time are not "real," but rather a simple psychological effect, a product of the material world. And while the business world has failed to accept that time is relative, the 80/20 individual, whether he or she realizes it or not, knows how to use time well.[1]

Time Is Not "Other"

Here are two themes that can help you twist your business idea into a unique shape. First, in business as in the rest of life, *time is not "other."* It is part of the physical things we make and provide to customers. It is part of our products, part of our services, part of our raw material, part of our output.

Therefore, we should not think of what we do for customers as separate from the time we take to do it. *We should not think of products or services on the one hand, and time on the other. We should think of "product-time" and "service-time."* Time is part of what we add or subtract.

Providing an existing product or service in a much faster way could change its economics and offer you a terrific new business opportunity.

Second, time is not finite and short, nor is it our enemy or a commodity in extremely short supply. Time is an integral part of what we do and who we are. Time is a dimension where, like space, we can express ourselves and create value for others, and therefore ourselves.

People living in a free society rarely say, "I don't have enough physical room to express myself; there is not enough space in my life." But people often do say, "I don't have enough time to express myself; I don't have enough time to do what I want." It sounds more plausible; it makes as little sense.

By combining the theories of Einstein and Pareto, you'll discover that *if 80 percent of the wealth (or anything else desirable) is created in less than 20 percent of the time available, then there is no shortage of time.* For individuals and business alike, there is no shortage of time. The problem is our trivial use of time, not time itself. We use our time most productively for only a small part of our existence; most of what we do matters little. In other words, our problem is triviality itself; few people achieve their full potential, or anywhere close to it.

Any venture or person could achieve much more while using much less time. The 80/20 principle suggests that you could work a two-day week and still achieve 60 percent more than you do now.

Einstein's theory reinforces the idea of the 20 percent spike and redefines it in terms of time. In other words, *the activities that make the very best use of our time must define our business and make it unique.*

Creating 80/20 Time

There are two steps you must take to create 80/20 product-time and service-time:

1 Compress the Delivery Time to Customers

A product or service delivered in half the time, or double the time, is not the same product or service. Delivering in less time will usually both cut costs and please customers—a double win that should be re-flected in higher margins.

❖ For any business you are in or might enter, identify the 20 percent of activities that take 80 percent of the time and the 20 percent that comprise 80 percent of your total cost (they are often the same).

❖ Work out what you would need to do to cut the time taken in half (for example, to service your restaurant's customers). Decide if the change is worthwhile and where it would lead.

❖ Then repeat the exercise (at least in your head) another three times. By cutting the time four times, it will be slashed to just over 6 percent of what it used to be. This 16-times improve-ment is what we should expect with the 80/20 principle (I will explain why in the next chapter).

❖ Decide if, as a result of these changes, costs would be signif-icantly lower or customer satisfaction higher. If so, make the changes. Make them hard for competitors to copy.

One way to cut the amount of time it takes to offer a product is self-service: a very old idea that still has terrific innovative power. The essence of self-service is that you delegate certain tasks—preferably the most expensive or time-consuming ones—to the customer.

Savvy carmakers and video game providers are involving cus-tomers in the design and testing of new products. ATMs enable cus-tomers to avoid lines, providing cash and other services much more quickly and much more cheaply than in traditional bank branches. Customers at fast-food chains replace the waitstaff. Smart consulting firms co-opt client personnel on projects, lowering costs and leaving the organization better equipped for the future because the client per-sonally understands the objectives of the new strategy.

Many retailers now provide customers with computer terminals so that they can find and order products without tying up salespeople. (The key is to provide *good* customer service with *as few* staff mem-bers as possible. Supermarkets that feature a "cashier-free" aisle are a brilliant example—the customers do most of the work!) Not all types of direct retailing (phone, fax, the Internet, and catalogs) speed up service delivery and cut costs, but many do.

The extent of self-service activity is constrained only by imagination. What might a self-service revolution in your business arena lead to?

Time may be compressed in many other ways. When I started in consulting, a typical project took nine months. When I hung up my consulting boots two decades later, it took three months.

I'm still not sure how we saved all this time. Technology and a greater availability of financial data certainly helped. More importantly, planning techniques developed by 80/20 individuals helped consultants focus on the key issues and reduce the huge amount of time "wasted" on a project—work that went down dead alleys and never made it into the final presentation shown to clients. Finally, increased competition and the willingness of consultants to "turn on a dime" for clients fundamentally sped up the clock.

Belgo, a restaurant chain that started in London in 1992 with my backing, is a great example of the importance of time. It became a successful chain of glitzy *moules-frites* emporia modeled on a monastery dining hall; waiters dressed as monks, and the menu featured two hundred different Belgian beers from obscure monasteries.

Belgo offered a fun meal in an expensively designed setting at a bargain price: "A $60-a-head experience at a $30-a-head price" was how one of my partners described it. It became very popular, and when we sold out on the stock market we made twenty times our original capital.

How could Belgo offer great value yet also be such a profitable venture? It was a matter of time compression. The Belgo system relied on turning the tables very quickly. Most restaurants have one or two sittings a night, but Belgo often achieved seven or eight. I joked to my partners that we appeared to own a fast-food restaurant (they were not amused, since they took the quality of the food very seriously).

Most restaurants in central locations have horrific fixed costs: large chunks of revenue go straight to rent, depreciation, and labor. *Such costs are related to time, not to volume.* Squeeze extra revenue out of a given site in a given time, and it drops straight to the bottom line.

In compressing time, Belgo violates many rules. Instead of being parsimonious with staff, it floods the place with waiters—more monks per square foot than you'd find in a monastery. Instead of encouraging diners to stay as long as they want, customers booking tables are told that they've a ninety-minute time slot, which encourages timely arrival.

Belgo provides extraordinarily prompt service. Drink orders are taken within one minute of customers arriving, food orders within three minutes, and the food comes within five minutes of ordering. A customized, automated ordering process and an open-plan kitchen that runs like clockwork support this delivery. Bills are presented with the last course or within fifteen minutes of the scheduled exit time. Credit cards are processed within a minute of being offered.

Belgo is a just-in-time factory. Many food critics, and some first-time customers, hate it. But many loyal customers return every week because Belgo provides a service they find valuable—quality meals provided cheaply and quickly. It is a fine example of 80/20 management—making better use of capital in ways that a segment of customers like and accept—and enjoys extraordinary returns: 80 percent of turnover and profit from 20 percent of capital input.

2 *Make a Detailed Plan to Cut Time*

❖ Draw up a physical map or plan of the steps necessary to deliver products and service to customers *measured against time.*

❖ Put a box around each step where the business does something to add value, ensuring that they are placed in sequence. Connect the boxes with arrows.

❖ In each box mark how much time it takes to complete each step. Record the time it typically takes to move from one step to the next one in the arrows connecting each box (see the accompanying chart as an example). Add up the total "box" time and the total "arrow" time.

Typical Restaurant	Belgo
seat clients **1 minute**	**seat clients** **& take drinks order** **2 minutes**
5 MINUTES	2 MINUTES
take drink order **2 minutes**	**take food order** **2 minutes**
10-15 MINUTES	0 MINUTES
take food order **2 minutes**	**cook food** **10 minutes**
10 MINUTES	1 MINUTE
cook food **20 minutes**	**deliver food** **1 minute**
5 MINUTES	25 MINUTES
deliver food **1 minute**	**provide bill &** **accept payment** **2 minutes**
25 MINUTES	
provide bill **1 minute**	Total Belgo Time: 45 minutes
10 MINUTES	
accept payment **1 minute**	
Total Typical Restaurant Time: 96 minutes	

FIGURE 2: Making a Plan to Cut Time

The chart demonstrates the two ways of speeding up delivery of your product or service. You could cut the time taken *in the boxes* by speeding up the activities you provide. Or you could cut the time *between the boxes.*

Typically, more time is taken between the boxes than within them. In other words, firms spend more time doing nothing than they do when doing something. A study by the Boston Consulting Group found that "typically, less than 10 percent of the total time devoted to any work in an organization is truly value-added. The rest is wasted because of unnecessary steps or unbalanced operations."[2]

At Belgo, the process of seating (time within the box) could be speeded up only by combining steps, such as showing patrons to their seats and then *immediately* taking their drinks order. But much more important was compressing the time between this "box" and the next one, which was taking the food order. By combining the two steps, Belgo reduced the standard restaurant seating and food-delivery time of 10–15 minutes to 2–3 minutes.

In consulting, the best way to compress time is *extensive upfront planning.* One terrific tool is the blank slide presentation, a guess at the start of a project as to what our final presentation would look like. As the work progressed, we either filled in each previously blank slide with a piece of the presentation, or discarded it as irrelevant, substituted another blank slide, and tried a new approach. This mechanistic exercise, oddly enough, stimulated rather than restricted creativity. It forced us to keep thinking about what the answer might be.

We discovered that the less time we had, the more important and urgent it was to start with the plan, and to devote a greater percentage of time to planning before acting.

Can you use time to refine your business idea and make your prospective venture more distinctive?

Make Time Subject to the 80/20 Principle

80/20 individuals are at the heart of any business. Similarly, the business must be at the heart of the 80/20 individual. An 80/20 individual is constantly on the lookout for ways his or her unique skills and ambitions can further benefit the company or department.

1 Identify Your Most Valuable Activities

For creative tasks, a small portion of time nearly always leads to most of the value created—for instance, the flash of insight that leads to a new scientific theory, or the idea for a new business.

If we had even a minor flash of insight once a month, we could multiply the wealth we create in that month many times over. It is worth thinking about how to stimulate such insights. How did earlier insights arise? In the office? Over lunch? Walking in the woods? In conversation with a particular person? Talking to customers? Playing golf? Whatever you were doing before, try spending more time on it and see if new insights arise.

By definition, rare flashes of insight cannot fill much of our time. It therefore becomes important to identify the routine activities that result in most of our productivity.

Think of a five-day workweek. If the 80/20 principle applies, work taking no more than eight hours—20 percent—generates 80 percent of the value. If you can isolate the high-value work activities and spend another day on them, without diminishing returns, two days should give you 160 percent of the previous value. In theory, two days of 80/20 work could be worth 60 percent more than five days of regular work.

Your high-value activities, for example, might be selling to important customers; discovering that a profitable customer is dissatisfied and correcting the problem; thinking up a new high-margin product; working out how to raise margins on existing products while keeping customers happy; hiring a superstar; letting go of someone whose standards are too low. These activities may take little time; each may create fantastic value.

You may choose to work five days, two on high-value activities and three on low-value ones. The numbers suggest that this would give you 175 percent of today's value.

A final benchmark would be to work five days on high-value activity, for 400 percent of the value. But you'd have to eliminate the low-value uses of your time. Either stop these activities, or get some-one else to do them.

2 Link Your High-Value Activities to Your New Idea

More important than the numbers is the *identity* of your wealth-creating activities, and their *relationship to your potential new venture.* Is your 20 percent spike—your unique, wealth-creating abilities—congruent with the way in which you are going to remodel an existing business or create a new one? The match is more crucial than you might imagine.

In chapter 4, I introduced Zoffany, my hotel business, and its unique mix of business ideas. The Zoffany formula is derived from its two leaders' 20 percent spikes. Niall Caven is a former investment banker who treats hotel acquisitions in the same way a private equity person would: Each new hotel must generate a high internal rate of return, which depends heavily on its initial purchase price. The development plan, which usually means building more bedrooms, must show a very high rate of return, too; the extent of development is driven by the numbers.

In contrast, Nick Sonley, the other Zoffany entrepreneur, is a brilliant hotelier who is best at coaching general managers to take responsibility for the happiness of guests and to maximize the profitability of their hotels. He is also skilled at designing and executing first-rate improvements and extensions at low cost, by carefully selecting and supervising local builders.

In (useful) management jargon, Zoffany's core competencies match those of its two 80/20 individuals. Caven and Sonley spend most of their time on the vital few areas where each excels. But time allocation is secondary to the strategy we crafted around their most vital uses of time. The unique and valuable aspects of Zoffany's business system match the unique and valuable traits of its leaders.

Belgo followed the same formula. It also had two founders, Denis Blais and André Plisnier. Blais and Plisnier were both wild enthusiasts of Belgian food and high-quality traditional "peasant" food. But while Blais's passion for design helped him create the unique Belgo look—the illusion of the monastery eating hall—Plisnier's experience as a bar and restaurant manager led to his understanding of the link between speed and profitability; he created the Belgo "factory" mentality and procedures. Although they could not confine their activities—at least in the early days—to the high-value ones, their unique areas of expertise certainly defined Belgo as a unique and high value restaurant.

When you define your own high-value activities, and those of your colleagues, you are creating 80/20 time. Moreover, you are devising a blueprint for your new idea. What makes you and your team unique wealth creators will also make your idea unique and successful.

Rachel: An 80/20 Case Study of a Manager

When I ask the ever-relaxed Rachel what her most valuable activities are, she immediately replies, "Design, margin management, marketing, and selecting my top team. I know what will work for each of my customer groups, which product will go with each brand. Because the team is so good, I have an easy time."

"Why do you say 'selecting' your team, not 'managing' or 'leading'?"

"Selecting, yes," she exclaims, "leading, yes, I suppose so; managing, no. They manage themselves. Leading means pointing in the right direction, but the ideas that drive us forward come from all members of the team; it's a collective thing. Look, the really valuable things we do are our ideas—ideas for new products, ideas for improved selling, ideas for lower-cost products, ways to manage our margins even better. I have ideas but so do Helena, and Georgina, and Bill, and many others. What I do is create the environment that brings forth masses of new ideas, and that then sorts the wheat from the chaff. If we agonize over a decision, I know we should reject the idea. The great ideas are always the easy ones, the ones that arise spontaneously, when we all say 'yes' right away."

Rachel spends pretty much all her time on high-value activities. As a result, she is rarely stressed and always has time to think. Not surprisingly, her key decisions are inspired. Making money is all about making the right decisions—and realizing when a decision is necessary. How much more value could you create if you were rarely pressured and always thought about the big decisions before a crisis loomed?

80/20 Individuals Use Time to Create Value

Time is a dimension of business, intimately related to the products and services offered and their economics, not an outside or separate entity.

Time is a dimension of ourselves, intimately related to the wealth we create and the unique attributes we have. Time is part of the 80/20 individual's tool kit; if you can learn and replicate something faster than others, you can do it better.

The ability to be extraordinarily productive in product-time, service-time, and entrepreneur-time is the basis of a superior business system. Speed and value are closely connected; speed alone often determines value. True value is defined by your ability to demonstrate results from your skill, and to do it quickly.

The unique abilities of 80/20 individuals and the businesses they create should be measured along the single dimension of time-value. Your new venture should offer a unique and superior package of time-value, one that nobody else could create.

CHAPTER 7

Hire Great Individuals

If I have seen further, it is by standing on the shoulders of giants.
—*Sir Isaac Newton*

E very venture capitalist knows that there is nothing more important in a new or young business than its people. That's all very
well in practice, but how does it work in theory?

The 80/20 principle tells us that there is an enormous difference
between the few, best performances and the rest—that fewer than 20
percent of any peer group will typically achieve 80 percent of its results.

Is this right? Does it fit with what we know about people and business success? And, right or wrong, what are the principal implications
of an empirically derived theory that nearly everyone is ignoring?

This chapter will help you come to truly astounding conclusions,
both thought and profit provoking.

Just How Valuable Is an 80/20 Individual?

How much better—in terms of adding value—would you expect the
best people to be compared to the rest? Fifty percent better? Twice as
valuable? Four times? If someone in your business were twice or four

times as valuable as another employee, it would clearly be worth paying a large premium to secure his or her services.

Yet the 80/20 principle suggests that the best 20 percent of any peer group is likely to be at least *16 times* as valuable as the other 80 percent.[1] Here's an explanation based on a group of 100 people.

If the most productive 20 percent produce 80 percent of the value, then one of the 20 most productive will produce, on average, 4 percent of the total (if 20 people produce 80 percent of value, divide 80 by 20 to get 4). And if the 80 percent of less productive people produce a total of 20 percent, each one of them will produce just 0.25 units: 20 divided by 80 = ¼.

Therefore, the ratio of productivity for the top 20 percent compared to the bottom 80 percent is divided by ¼ = 16 times.

This can be expressed as follows:

Vital group (20%) $\quad \dfrac{80\% \text{ results}}{20\% \text{ people}} \quad = 4.00$

Trivial group (80%) $\quad \dfrac{20\% \text{ results}}{80\% \text{ people}} \quad = 0.25$

Ratio of vital group
to trivial group $\qquad\qquad = \dfrac{4.00}{0.25} = 16$

Is a Difference of 16 Times Credible?

Differences in measurable intelligence follow a bell curve, not an 80/20 distribution. The top-20-percent-of-intelligence people are not twice as intelligent as the rest, let alone 16 times brighter. So does this mean that the 80/20 principle is not applicable to IQ?

Yes and no. Clearly the 80/20 principle does not apply to intelligence, and therefore not to talent, which is a form of intelligence. However, those of us interested in success and the creation of economic wealth and well-being should not be interested in talent per se. Talent is a wonderful thing, but unless it leads to the creation of wealth and well-being, it doesn't concern us here.

In the interest of success in economics, the 80/20 principle—with its counterintuitive, often offensive, and even outrageous results—is what works. The 80/20 principle arose from an academic study of economics, not because it formed some convenient bridge in an economist's theory, but because it was observable in so many economic phenomena.

As economist Josef Steindl remarked: "For a very long time, the Pareto law [the 80/20 principle] has lumbered the economic scene like an erratic block on the landscape, an empirical law which nobody can explain."[2]

Vilfredo Pareto's original discovery, which led to the 80/20 principle, was based on observations of incomes and wealth over many time periods and many countries. The consistency of observation led him to the algebra behind the principle.[3]

A century of egalitarian tax policies has not been able to overturn the 80/20 principle's sway over income distributions. The top 10 percent of the world's population receive 70 percent of its total income and produce 70 percent of its goods and services.[4] In the United States, the top 5 percent own as much market wealth as the bottom 60 percent.[5] The wealthiest 20 percent of Americans own 83.9 percent of the country's wealth.[6]

The increasing wealth created by superstars in the entertainment and sports industries as well as by the industries themselves, at the relative expense of less successful professionals and industries, proves the tenacity of the 80/20 principle.[7]

Koch's Law of Individual Wealth Creation

So how do we reconcile psychology and economics, the bell curve and the 80/20 distribution? Both arose empirically; both are well proven.

The answer is crystal clear. *The bell curve and the 80/20 principle refer to different things. The bell curve refers to intelligence and talent; and the 80/20 principle refers to the capacity of individuals to generate wealth and well-being.*

Two insights follow:

❖ Talent is not enough. Talent is useless if it doesn't create wealth or well-being. *We should therefore ask what alchemy converts talent to wealth-making.*

❖ Contrary to our expectations—and even perhaps to our sense of what is right and proper—the 80/20 principle does refer to the wealth-creating power of individuals. The mathematics of the 80/20 principle apply. *The wealth creators create at least 16 times more than the rest of the population.*

Michael Jordan is not 16 times more intelligent than other players. He is not even 16 times better on the field. Yet his ability to create wealth exceeds other players' by 16 times.

By translating talent into wealth creation, and converting psychology into economics, economic leverage occurs. Small differences in talent are multiplied into large differences in wealth-creating capacity.

Koch's Law of Individual Wealth Creation helps explain why:

Wealth = (Talent) × (Wealth Creation Multiple)

Of these two variables, the wealth creation multiple is more important. Because it clearly varies more than talent does, the wealth creation multiple is vital.

What Is the Wealth Creation Multiple?

I'll return to our friends from chapter 4, the powerful business genes. The ideas and vehicles that constitute vital packets of economic power, that convert a level playing field into Michael Jordan's court, a stadium into a Madonna concert, a book into a John Grisham bestseller.

I'll re-state my own Law of Individual Wealth Creation:

Wealth = (Talent) × (Business Genes)

Intelligence does not translate into wealth. If it did, college professors would all be millionaires. Many people wonder why certain business folks become so wealthy, even if they're less intelligent than their peers. It can't be explained by hard work: Many people work hard and never become rich. And while luck plays a large role, it's only a word applied to something we cannot explain or influence.

The answer lies in powerful business genes. Although people often stumble across these by sheer luck, there is a crucial difference between the supersuccessful and the rest. Whether intuitively or deliberately, successful people latch on to powerful business genes.

In the past this may have been largely intuitive. Now, by decoding the science of success, we can engineer the process more deliberately.

Some business genes are more powerful—create more wealth—than others. Before long, we should be able to study and quantify the genes that possess a higher wealth creation multiple objectively.[8]

How to Turn Talent into Wealth

Talent turns into wealth when brought into contact with powerful business genes that can use the talent for their purposes.

Which is the better bargain: talent or mediocrity? Let's run some numbers; imagine a peer group filled with talented and mediocre people with equal motivation.

Assume that the talented minority of a peer group have a skill quotient of 120, while the mediocre majority have a quotient of 80. To attract the talented few, assume we would have to pay not 50 percent more (the "fair" reflection of their worth), but 70 percent more.

To some extent, motivation and talent balance each other. Nevertheless, you can reasonably assume that you'll want to hire highly motivated people. Incidentally, many mediocre people are highly motivated, which makes it difficult sometimes to spot their mediocrity. It is easier to notice and screen out talented people whose interest in your business is only skin-deep.

On the surface, under these conditions, only a fool would buy talent. Talent appears overpriced.

But Koch's Law of Individual Wealth Creation suggests another variable is at work: the business genes used to convert talent into wealth. While the multiple affects both talent and mediocrity, is it reasonable to assume that both talent and mediocrity will make equal use of the powerful business gene? Will both groups milk it for all it is worth? Or will the talented group be better positioned to grasp the essence of the powerful business gene? Will they make 10 times the use of it that the mediocre group does? In other words, will the business gene make 10 times better use of a talented person than of a mediocre person?

If so, the results would be as follows:

$$\text{Value of mediocre individual} = 80 \times 1 = 80$$
$$\text{Value of talented individual} = 120 \times 10 = 1{,}200$$

In this case, the talented individual will produce output worth 15 times (1,200/80) that of the mediocre individual, despite being less than twice as intelligent.

Is this credible? Possibly. I have chosen the "10 times" factor—the use that the talented person makes of a powerful business gene—quite arbitrarily. You may or may not find this plausible.

Note this, however. The calculation above says that a talented individual may produce 15 times more value than someone mediocre. This is close to the 16-times factor implied by the 80/20 principle. Although my reasoning is circular, a relationship similar to the proven 80/20 principle may apply. My calculation's accuracy depends on whether the weights I attach to talent and to the business gene "x factor" are correct.

Of course, this multiple of 10 applies only to an *average* of powerful business genes. In some cases the business genes may be less powerful, and only give a multiple of, say, 5. At the tail of the distribution the multiplying power of the business gene may be very high indeed, in the hundreds or thousands in extreme cases.

While these numbers are theoretical, I can say with certainty that individuals such as Bill Gates and Warren Buffett create millions of times more value (as measured by the capital markets) than do most of us. And it is not that they are millions of times smarter. Their genius lies in finding and using the very best ideas to create wealth in their particular domains. You could do the same.

Even if Einstein had an IQ of 200 or 300, the genes he replicated— the scientific ideas that made up the raw material of relativity theory—must have been extraordinarily powerful, way above average.

The concept of genius, that some human beings are very much more intelligent than others, cannot explain the astronomical power of the results that a genius produces. The explanation must lie in leverage. Genius, whether in science or business, lies in *finding and exploiting* powerful business genes. Differences in intelligence become multiplied in their effects.

How to Spot and Hire Great 80/20 Individuals

1 **Understand the Practical Implications of the Law of Individual Wealth Creation**

Hiring talent is a much better deal than hiring mediocrity. In my example, people possessing 50 percent more talent than their peers were paid 70 percent more. In my calculation, talented individuals produced 15 times more value than their peers.

Assume that a mediocre person costs 50 units and a talented person 85 units (70 percent more).

The return on a mediocre individual = 80/50 = 1.6.

The return on a talented individual = 1,200/70 = 17.1, more than 10 times the return on the mediocre person.

Talent turns into wealth creation only when powerful business genes are applied. To some extent, new talent itself drives this process. But to a much larger extent, new talent is the beneficiary of business genes, as the process of exploiting them to produce valuable results has already been worked out by an earlier generation of talented wealth creators—and is already crystallized within a particular industry, corporation, or team.

This explains why newborn talent is not yet able to command its output value. In fact, talent does not, initially, deserve its output value. The value derives from talent's interaction with powerful business genes already available within the industry and corporation—business genes that are more important than the talent.

Imagine two freshly minted MBAs, George and Susan, start working for a management consulting firm on the same day. While both are very bright, George has better grades than Susan.

The key requirements for success as a consultant are the abilities to get along well with client personnel, and to organize a team to produce work quickly—these are the "business genes." Susan is a natural at both. She quickly learns what to say and not say to clients, and how to motivate the junior analysts reporting to her. As a result, her teams are popular with clients and produce the work on budget and on time. This is how management consulting firms make their money.

George's intelligence proves to be a handicap in the consulting world. He always chases after fascinating ideas that are intellectually satisfying but fail to improve the bottom line. His quirks make him difficult to work for. As a result, his teams are unmotivated and sometimes late and over budget with their reports. George is also a bit aloof with clients, unless he feels they are as smart as he is. George has buckets of talent and intelligence, but no handle on the business formula that drives profitability in the consulting industry.

Employees who work effectively with powerful business genes may be able to parlay those ideas, with some individualistic tweaking, into a successful new venture—thus becoming 80/20 individuals.

2 Exploit the Theory of Wealth/Talent Arbitrage

Talent is not difficult to spot. Grab it before your competitors do, and convert it into wealth-creating capacity as quickly and fully as possible. Recruit the type of talent that is most likely to make the leap to wealth creation quickly.

Talent creates wealth when fused with powerful business genes. To start with, talent has little value. But given time, talent can have considerable or great value independent of its employer. Talent accumulates value as it assimilates and becomes useful to powerful business genes. Exceptional wealth creators learn to import all the valuable business genes used by their employees, predecessors, and competitors.

More than a matter of general talent, wealth creation combines motivation with the only type of talent that matters: instincts for spotting the vital few business genes and knowing how to use them better than anyone else. In my experience, however, it is extremely difficult to assess an employee's motivation, or whether their talent will necessarily turn into wealth generation. However, it will show up in results.

Talent rarely gets paid fairly. At the very beginning of its career, talent is overpaid. But before long, if talent mutates into wealth-creating ability, it will be underpaid.

The price of wealth creators depends on reputation and self-confidence. The two go together, but are far from perfectly correlated. To observe this, enter any bar just before closing time. Reputation rarely equals an employee's wealth-creating capacity. In the early years of a truly exceptional wealth creator, her ability to create wealth exceeds her reputation. In the later years, with few exceptions, once she's proven herself, it's the other way around.

3 Appreciate the Value of Young Talent

80/20 individuals snap up young talent with wealth-creation potential before that potential is appreciated. The talented are converted, as quickly as possible, into wealth creators. At this stage the 80/20 employer has gotten a great bargain because wealth creators must, by definition, be many times—on average, 16 times—more effective than the merely competent majority. Therefore, 80/20 individuals take great pains to coach and develop talented young people to absorb the powerful business genes and become living exemplars of the 80/20 principle. If some of the talented people do not turn into wealth creators, the 80/20 manager has made a hiring error and must correct it.

The value of young talent is still greater than its price, although the gap for some types of talent is narrowing. For example, new business graduates (MBAs) from Massachusetts Institute of Technology were paid 60 percent more in 1998 than in 1994, while the earnings of forty-five- to fifty-four-year-old male college graduates over the past quarter century actually fell (in inflation-adjusted dollars) by 24 percent.[9] The young are getting more expensive, the old are losing value. Still, in value terms, the young are often cheaper than their salaries reveal, given their fresh enthusiasm to import the most powerful business genes and ferret out new ones.

Long-term employees may have chosen their own path. More often than not, they remained employees because they failed to become wealth generators, failed to realize that they were wealth generators, or failed to keep a fair share of the wealth they created. The many people who fall into the last two categories are extremely important exceptions. You may be one of them. If so, much of this book is written for those of you who have learned to generate wealth but have yet to gain the money and control over your lives it should bring. You are failing to keep what is rightfully yours!

When one pool of talent becomes expensive, switch to another pool that possesses the same characteristics, but is in much less demand.

MBA students used to be good value; now they are overpriced. And while the British were once courted heavily, the transatlantic brain-drain has stopped flowing for many good reasons. Freshly minted college graduates used to be a fantastic value; now they are merely cheap. I advise you to hire extremely bright employees who lack experience, graduates in unfashionable subjects (such as the humanities), dropouts, eighteen-year-olds who perform well on objective tests, or executives from countries that have excellent higher education programs, but pay poorly (such as India, South Africa, or New Zealand).

Avoid talent pools that your competitors frequent. Your competitors are any firms that have business genes—the ability to convert talent to wealth—that are as good as or better than yours.

Determine the conversion rate of talent to wealth creation for each talent pool. Compare this value to the cost you pay and recruit accordingly.

You should always pay wealth generators more than they expect and less than they are worth. This should leave a wide margin for appropriating a fat surplus. Be generous early, before it is too late.

Finally, raise the average moneymaking capacity, or potential capacity, in the firm with each new hire. Many bosses tend to hire people with whom they feel comfortable, who won't challenge their superiority. This is a big mistake. For positive arbitrage, hire the very best people you can find, especially if they are better than you or might become bet-

ter than you. Hire only people who have the potential to be your partner. Even if they eventually leave, you'll benefit immensely from them.
   In sum:

* Hire the type of young talent that can become wealth generators quickly.
* Of these, hire the cheapest; if you look in the right places,
  you may be able to hire brilliant people for moderate pay.
* For any given level of talent and wealth-creation potential,
  favor the underconfident and beware of the overconfident.
  The former are likely to stay longer after they have become
  powerful wealth generators.
* Overpay young wealth creators who have successfully completed the wealth-creation apprenticeship. Qualified appren-
  tices are always terrific value, even when they are overpaid.
  Lock them in.
* Help talented people who fail to become wealth generators
  find a great job in another firm, where they can be overpaid
  by your competitors.
* Be careful to spot, hire, and nurture older employees who are
  genuine wealth creators, but fail to realize or capitalize on
  their value.
* Hire to raise the bar in your department no matter how high
  it is already. Hire people whose potential ability to create
  wealth is greater than yours.

How to Lock in Great People

Being openhanded early on creates maximum personal loyalty. You
can afford to be generous with a young wealth creator; you're almost
certainly getting a better deal than he or she is.

When Bill Bain was boss of the eponymous management consultancy, he made a habit of making his young superstars "partners"
about a year before they could reasonably expect it. He told them
about the appointment six months in advance, in order to boost their

motivation level some time before he had to pay for it; six months is a long time in consulting. Those of us who were the beneficiaries felt enormously grateful to Bain. The only cost to him was an early decision. The "partners" tended to overlook the fact that they held only tiny shares of the partnership, and that Bain held on to most of the equity.

When you wish to lock in genuine partners, it pays to be generous with the equity. Give the prospective partner a higher share than he or she expects—perhaps even more than he or she deserves—especially if the partner-designate is younger, less experienced, or has yet to reach full potential. Wealth-creating ability is a moving target; a partner's equity share is usually not. Overshoot now and you'll still be in the money.

When Jim Lawrence proposed creating a partnership with Iain Evans to form what became the LEK Partnership, Lawrence offered an equal stake to Evans even though he reported to Lawrence and was substantially less senior. At the time that decision seemed overly generous; in hindsight it was one of the best decisions Lawrence ever made.

Money matters a great deal but so do friendship and fun. I hold the controversial view that you should hire only people whom you like and who like you.

Fun is important for economic as well as noneconomic reasons. Fun is a good investment. Fun works. It has a high return on capital, even a high return on management effort. Fun is a bargain.

I don't mean that you should take everyone out for expensive meals (not often, anyway) or engage in frivolity. I do mean that you should build recreation time—both individual and social—into your division's work schedule. When work stops being fun, you should find out why and do something about it. If you think you can't afford to, you're not running an 80/20 enterprise. If you are making proper use of the 80/20 principle, you should be highly profitable despite paying top rates and having time for fun.

As Rachel told me, "Work can be boring and serious, or it can be fun. When I go to the head office, all that corporate stuff really is so tedious. All those long faces and frowns and formal meetings. When I get back here [to her office], it's different. I can express myself, we can all express ourselves. We do all the fun things together. We like each other. We make sure we have a good time. I don't feel guilty about it or think it's inappropriate. If we didn't get on so well we wouldn't keep raising the profits year after year."

The Virtuous Cycle of Hiring—and Keeping—Employees

Once you have a core group of great employees, you've entered a virtuous cycle. Your firm's reputation is enhanced, so it becomes easier to attract other great wealth creators. You'll boost morale, productivity, and profitability. These attributes in turn make it easier still to enlist even stronger wealth creators. They in turn add to profits, which allows the firm to reinvest in what produces the profits . . . and so on, unless you become complacent, arrogant, or unlucky.

If you sense the momentum of the virtuous cycle faltering, the first leading indicator won't be a drop in sales or profits—it will be the departure of some of your outstanding people. To lose one or two is okay, but any more is no coincidence; it's a warning. Only immediate extreme measures will keep the virtuous cycle from spinning in reverse.

What to Do If Great Employees Leave

If one or two excellent people leave, hire some more people with great potential. Don't just aim to raise the firm's average; hire people with potential to be better than those who have left. Before long, this should raise your profitability.

If more than a few leave, panic. Find out why. Don't accept the polite answer. Probe for the real reasons. Talk to your other best people. Ask for their recommendations. Do everything they ask of you, and more.

The Value of Oddballs

The theories of natural selection and of business genes tell us that, in business as in life, the key ingredient is diversity. Diversity becomes efficiency. Homogeneity leads to death.[10]

Most people do not like too much diversity, especially in their colleagues. They like people who are like them. But good 80/20 managers challenge themselves to recruit from a diverse population.

Deliberately seek out recruitment candidates from unusual backgrounds—whatever is unusual for your firm: ethnic minorities, gays, foreigners, poor people, rich people, underqualified people, overqualified people, cultured people, street-smart people—and make it a rule that one new hire in three (or two, or four) has to be from an "unusual" background.

Make your venture a beacon, if not to the huddled masses, then at least to the vital few among them: a refuge for truly talented and motivated people from unconventional backgrounds, people who would not normally get a break in your business. Bill Bain's a great example. When he was hired by Bruce Henderson in the early days of the Boston Consulting Group, Bill had no business degree; in fact, he knew nothing about business.[11] He had been a Bible salesman and a college official raising funds from alumni. Yet he went on to become consulting's biggest individual wealth generator for a generation.

Whether we like it or not—and I personally do—affirmative action works. So does immigration. Without wave upon wave of immigrants, America and Europe would be much less wealthy. So encourage "immigration" of unusual, unique people—even the occasional oddball—to your team. But realize that immigration is never an easy process and needs to be *managed*. Make sure that there is enough affinity between the new hire and your existing staff for the mix to work. Even your "oddballs" must be fully integrated into the firm's normal processes, rather than being stranded on an island of eccentricity.

The Theory of the Tribe

The new field of evolutionary psychology[12] says that while business conditions have changed enormously since the Stone Age, humans have not. Few of us behave rationally when it comes to our workplace; it's much more accurate to say that we are quivering masses of emotion, looking for a tribe to belong to and our natural place in its pecking order.

We herd. We conform. We want someone else to lead us. We are friendly to those inside the tribe and suspicious of those outside. We avoid risk. We reject criticism of ourselves. We jump to conclusions based on first impressions. Above all, we want to identify with a small tribe, of no more than 150 people, whom we can know by face and name. In the Stone Age these attributes worked: They facilitated survival. Today they are often a trap.

The tribe is generally a department or other subunit that has frequent face-to-face interaction and a common purpose. If you are starting a new business, however, the tribe should be, and usually is, the whole firm.

What are the implications for 80/20 managers?

- ❖ Everybody wants a cohesive tribe and you must create one—the people must like each other and work well together.
- ❖ You will find it easier to entice people out of their existing corporations if their need for a tribe can be better met in your company. If they are happy in their current tribe, it will be virtually impossible to dislodge them.
- ❖ If the people you want to join your new venture are already happy together in your existing firm, that is a very strong reason for dealing with your corporation on a joint venture or other hybrid solution (see chapter 8).
- ❖ The ideal scenario for a leader wanting to set up a new independent venture occurs when the tribe in your existing company starts begging for you to lead them. To found a spinoff, lead from behind and wait until everyone is ready.
- ❖ Exploit tribalism. Happy tribes stick together. People on the

edge of the tribe have at least one foot outside the door already. If you want to keep someone who is not fitting in, take pains to integrate them: Ensure that they have at least a couple of colleagues with whom they click.

The Primacy and Power of Partners

Don't imagine that you are immune to the need for a tribe. All leaders and senior managers get lonely, because they are structurally cut off, at least to some degree, from everyone else. The only way to be happy as well as successful is to have at least one excellent partner. You need someone who complements your skills, but, more important, is a trusted soul mate: somebody with whom you share all your wild dreams, all your doubts, and all the ups-and-downs and twists-and-turns of the roller coaster that comprises business innovation.

Don't start an enterprise without at least one partner. I can't think of a successful and happy 80/20 individual, among the hundreds I have known, who didn't have at least one close business partner. In contrast, I can think of several control freaks who don't have a partner. While some of them are successful, none appears happy or fulfilled.

The ideal number of partners falls between two and seven. With groups of more than seven, intimacy is lost and cliques begin to form.

Partners are the most vital, the fewest, of the vital few. And when you are in business with real partners, make the most of it. Take business meetings and trips together, even if this seems inefficient. Visit each partner's house (or invite them to yours) at least once a week. Keep renewing your sense of partnership. Nothing is more precious, nor more essential, for professional success and happiness.

Venture DNA

There is much loose talk today about the "DNA" of particular firms. It is a more apt metaphor than most of its users know. Firms are unique not merely because of the mix of people within them, but because of the business genes within them. In fact, the business genes often stick around longer than the people do.

Teams, firms, industries, and markets are living entities that seethe with life. The life comprises a heady brew where ideas and people collide, compete, and collaborate. Effective firms, industries, and markets work because they are based on good ideas and good people that fit well with each other.

Like natural selection, the process is evolutionary and unpredictable. There must be constant variation, improvement, rejection of the majority of variants, and elaboration of the minority of successful variants.

If you are successful, it is because a great business gene has hitched a ride with you and likes the road you're taking. But watch the signs; the moment great business genes spot a smoother, faster ride to prosperity, they'll be out the door. If all your great individual wealth creators slip out with the business genes, thinking they can do better outside than inside your business, your ride is over.

Keeping the right people connecting with the right genes, with each other and you, is tricky. Humility, shrewdness, creativity, calculation, luck, experimentation, friendliness, realism, the ability to cooperate with the best cooperators—all of these are necessary to keep your team's DNA alive and well.

Keep Tabs on the Best 80/20 Individuals

There is one further point 80/20 managers should know about hiring great individuals. The link between young moneymakers and their more experienced counterparts can be invaluable. The patron/protégé relationship is important, not only in one firm, but over time, throughout business relationships. Once the younger person is taught how to exploit powerful business genes, he or she gains confidence, and rapidly learns how to create value. In the early stages, greater value passes to the protégé; soon, this coworker is adding much more value than he or she takes. At some stage the younger person either becomes a partner in the business or is likely to depart for a business that offers a substantial ownership stake. But the story doesn't end here.

Anton and Jamie were protégés of mine from LEK Consulting. They have since started their own ventures; Anton in the fulfillment of direct sales orders and Jamie in venture capital (I introduced Jamie in chapter 3). We stay in close touch and continue to add great value to each other. We swap investment opportunities, leads on business opportunities, and, most important of all, leads on talented people who can become moneymakers for us.

For example, Alex used to work for Marion, and they respect and like each other. Although he has moved to an investment banking firm where he manages a team of security analysts, when he needs another bright young analyst, he asks Marion if she knows anyone suitable. She then asks *her* former boss, who works on Wall Street. Together they find someone ideal for Alex's job. Another time, Marion needed a new computer but didn't know which one to buy. Alex sent his technical wizard to talk to Marion and recommend the right PC for her needs. With each favor executed and loosely reciprocated, they're weaving a stronger web of mutual support.

As do most 80/20 individuals, we've started a chain of mutual person-to-person benefit that will probably still be going strong long after the three of us have retired. This is the model for value creation in the future economy; a club of individuals helping each other find and exploit ideas to create wealth regardless of corporate affiliation.

Rachel: An 80/20 Case Study of a Manager

One reason Rachel fascinates me—and, I hope, you—is that although she has created enormous value by leading a business and remodeling it from scratch, she is a *manager*. Why hasn't she taken the initiative to start her own business, or redefine the terms of engagement with her corporation?

When I talk to her about this, she is ambivalent. On the one hand, she says, "I hate having this very successful business and yet being inside a corporation that is so spectacularly unsuccessful at everything else." On the other hand, she is reluctant to leave the corporate womb.

In 2001 she became part of a management buyout team. The initiative for the MBO came from her boss and a private equity firm. However, as the manager in charge of the most valuable part of the company, she was positioned to make $10 million or so in three years if the MBO worked out. In exchange, she had to invest $60,000 in the deal and undertake some legal "warranties."

Rachel went along with the MBO but hated the uncertainties and the twists and turns of the buyout process itself. At the last minute the deal was pulled, for reasons unrelated to Rachel or her business. Was she disappointed? "A bit," she answers, "but relieved is nearer the mark. I don't want to go through that process again.

"Management buyouts," she continues, "are all very well if all you're interested in is money. Well, I'm not. I like money, but I have enough of it already. What is important to me is the quality of my life—my working life and my nonworking life. My working life depends on the people I work with. I don't want to report to venture capitalists again."

Everything she says may be true, but I had to ask again: Is she really happy with the deal she and the team have today? I remind her of the wealth they've created, compared to their compensation. Aren't they getting shortchanged? Never mind the money itself; isn't it unfair?

"My team feels it's unfair. They could earn more elsewhere but we like working together. Millions and millions of dollars . . . it's not something they think they can get. They're not keyed into the financial community. They don't get exposed to those opportunities.

"Look, they were excited by the MBO, and very disappointed when it went away. They were also upset that no one from the executive office apologized. I was relieved because I felt it was all going to be my responsibility, that all the profits would have to be generated by me. I would feel responsible for Jason's mortgage and Jayne's children's education and all the rest if anything went wrong. The private equity people behind the deal made no attempt to get to know me and reassure me. Faced with a choice between venture capitalists and the status quo, I prefer the latter."

I tell Rachel there is a third option, one I'll tell you about in the next chapter.

CHAPTER 8

Use Your Current Company to Your Advantage

*No matter where you work, you are not an employee. You are
in business with one employer—yourself. . . .
Nobody owes you a career—you own it as a sole proprietor.*

—*Andy Grove, CEO, Intel Corporation*

B y now you should know the play and the cast: the way you will
remodel part of your current company, or the new business you
will create and the partners you'll choose. But where? Should you leave
your current company or stay within it?

The 80/20 principle can help you decide by guiding you to a very
profitable business, one where the return on capital is very high. If you
have learned how to create extraordinary value—perhaps after at-
tempting a dummy run in your existing firm—you would be shortchanging yourself to remain there. Your firm is almost certainly
exploiting you.

An 80/20 individual inside someone else's corporation will typically produce returns for the corporation that are between 20 and 200
times his or her compensation.[1] You can load yourself up with stock
options and bonuses, but rarely do ordinary corporations pay 80/20
individuals what they are worth. And the better you are at creating
wealth using the 80/20 principle, the more acute this problem will become.

In order to receive reasonable value—to enjoy a relationship between value creation and value capture that does not insult you—you

might find it difficult to stay at your current company. Once you realize how much you have to offer, it is a short hop to concluding that you should leave the firm and start your own business. Yet this conclusion is a purely economic one. And no decision on whether to stay or go will be—or should be—purely economical. Social and personal considerations also apply. Maybe you like your place of work and your coworkers. Maybe they couldn't or wouldn't join you in the new venture. Maybe you don't like the risk and hassle involved in going it alone.

Happily, you may be able to have your monetary cake and still enjoy the social experience of eating it. The choice is not exclusively between the alternatives of staying or leaving. In defiance of traditional physics and management theory, you may be able to do both.

The Incubator Deal for Managers

One permanent legacy from the "Internet bubble" of 1998–2000 has been the creation of "incubator" deals, where managers inside a company who have a bright idea receive funding to create a new business venture, but retain partial ownership. Such deals can work for managers in any company, regardless of whether technology is involved.

One 80/20 individual whom I'll call Jerry tells how it worked for him.[2]

"A group of friends and I working in the same company had decided that our idea had enormous value. We'd written a business proposal with the help of two Wall Street analysts we knew. We didn't have enough money and were tapping friends and family for support, when our firm decided to set up an incubator.

"The incubator is set up as a separate department within the company. People like us with ideas rub shoulders with venture capitalists, who test our new plans. We keep in touch with experts inside our old firm, and the firm takes a third of the shares in the new company we set up. The venture capitalists own about another third, and so do we—as long as we perform according to our plan.

"The incubator deal was good for us and also good for our former employer," says Jerry. "Without the incubator we would have left and started a totally separate business. They [the employer] would have been left with nothing. But with the help we get from them, and support in finding the money, it was worth us giving them [the employer] 33 percent of our venture. They have been very useful helping us with technical advice, and they do all the marketing for us as well. We have access to their customer base—so with their help our business can be bigger. We get a smaller share but the cake is larger and there is more security than there would have been if we'd gone out totally on our own."

The incubator model—whether it is called that or not—fits any business, whether it is high-tech, low-tech, or no-tech. It can give 80/20 individuals what they want, without forcing you to "leave" your companies or even your workmates. There does not even have to be an "incubator" for you to use this model. You can simply propose a similar deal to your current company.

Rick: An 80/20 Case Study in Banking

In the movie *The Firm,* Wilfred Brimley plays William Devasher, the crooked law firm's security chief, with powerful malevolence. But in proof that life imitates art, I'll tell you about my American friend Rick Haller, who bears an uncanny physical resemblance to Devasher/Brimley.

I was a BCG consultant when I first met Haller back in 1979. He was heading the merchant banking operation at Libra Bank, a consortium of leading world banks set up to exploit lending to Latin America. Haller is a true 80/20 individual, a natural wealth creator: He set up the merchant banking operation in Libra from scratch, and by 1980 it was making about $25 million in profits, with a return on average capital employed between 50 and 100 percent.

When I first interviewed him, Haller was open about his belief that his deal with Libra was unsatisfactory: "Here I am making all this money for them, while I just draw a decent salary. This is not fair compensation, but with our shareholders and all their red tape it would take years to sort it out."

Haller's opportunity to leave, with some twenty of the top fellow wealth creators in his team, came in 1980 when the shareholders decided to dismember Libra. To my surprise, Haller asked for my advice when setting up his new venture.

His problem was that his group needed some lines of capital to support its debt-trading operation—far more than he and his friends could raise. He also needed the respectability of an established banking base, so that other banks would accept him as a counterparty. But he was clear about what he wanted: total autonomy for his group, and a significant share of the profits.

He got it. He constructed a deal with a blue-chip investment bank. The emerging markets division was set up as a "bank within a bank," and Haller's group shared 23 percent of the annual profits while providing none of the capital. I estimate that his group made hundreds of millions of dollars' profit between 1980 and 1998, when Haller left the bank.

As a manager working in a large corporation, if you have an idea for a new business that would contribute an additional profit stream to your current company, nothing should stop you from proposing a deal similar to Haller's. But do not raise the matter until your plans are fully fledged. Without your having to say it, your employer should realize that if the firm does not give you what you want, you can reach your goals by making a deal with another similar firm.

Hold Out for the Best Deal

Richard, a successful investment banker based in London, worked for one investment bank, moved to another, then joined another as managing director. He loved making corporate finance deals but hated the administrative duties that came with being the boss. He therefore moved on to another bank where, around 1990, I first had a serious conversation with him about starting his own business.

Although he recognized that he created a lot of value, and that by setting up his own shop he could keep all the profits, in the end he decided not to. His reasoning was as follows: "I'm not sure the time is right. If I can pull off a couple of the huge deals I'm working on, then the timing would be better. Besides, I have my doubts about corporate finance boutiques. At the end of the day, clients like advice, but they like money better. They want to be able to finance deals, to have underwriting. Banks with capital can do that at a stroke. A boutique has to go looking."

However, before long Richard moved again, back to the second bank he had worked for. "But this time the deal is different," he told me. "I get to keep a high proportion of the profits I generate."

Richard's experience shows that moneymakers can work with an employer but strike their own deals. You don't need to have a team, as my friend Rick did. You can work on your own provided that you can generate profits yourself. This is most transparent in investment banking and corporate finance, but the economic system changes when the same principle is extended to other businesses.

Are Consulting Firms Models for the Future?

The consulting industry, where I spent my youth, provides several different ways in which firms reward their moneymakers. I find them interesting because the issues faced by consulting firms and their owners may offer a taste of what to expect in most businesses. Consultants are classic "knowledge workers" who are—in theory—mobile. Consultants can easily take the intellectual property of their previous firm; doing so is unavoidable. No matter what your industry is, if you want to be part of a new venture, you can learn from consultants about the nature of equity and the rewards necessary to motivate both entrepreneurs and employees.

How to Expropriate the Owners

When Bruce Henderson set up the Boston Consulting Group in 1963, he made a deal with the Boston Safe and Deposit Company, which provided the modest working capital needed to launch BCG. In the early 1970s, when BCG was already a raging success, a conflict arose between the value creators within the business and the bank that owned it. The solution was for BCG professionals to buy the company with its own cash flow, setting up an employee stock option plan (ESOP) for their entire professional staff.

In effect, BCG is now run as a professional partnership, sharing the profits among its staff while retaining a significant portion of each year's profits, to pay out over time as they "vest" for individuals. That way, BCG maintains working capital for expansion (and to cushion the occasional poor year) while using the earned (but not vested) portion of pay to encourage its best professionals to stay. The senior vice presidents at BCG make attractive sums of high six-figures in an average year and low seven-figures in great years, but are prevented from grabbing the instant millions that would result from selling the firm.

Who Should Own Knowledge Firms like Consultancies?

When a professional firm is sold, some partners can make tens of millions of dollars in one fell swoop. For example, Goldman Sachs floated in 1999 and, as I write, is worth $43 billion. More than 60 percent of that belongs to insiders.

Interestingly, Bruce Henderson chose to take only very modest returns from BCG. He was a passionate believer in the free market, but not for himself. He had no regrets, taking great pride in its profound influence and international expansion.

"When he set up BCG," senior vice president Barry Jones told me, "Bruce did an extraordinary thing. Rather than keep the equity for himself he gave it to the employees. He created BCG as an inverted pyramid, as a flat structure. As a partner of eighteen years, my share of the equity is only twice that of a new partner."

In splitting off from BCG in 1970, Bill Bain pursued a different model. Right until his withdrawal from the business in 1990, he retained ownership of a majority of Bain & Company's equity. When the market was up the firm was sold to its professional staff, who funded the deal with a boatload of debt, just in time for a market downturn. Despite its terrific business formula and excellent work, Bain's future had hung in the balance for several months. It is now effectively a partnership like BCG and McKinsey.

McKinsey is a most interesting case. Insiders claim that without the lingering influence of Marvin Bower, McKinsey's leader between 1937 and 1960, the firm would have gone public in the 1990s, as younger partners lobbied for a deal that would make their fortunes. But Bower's stern rectitude blocked a deal. After all, in 1963, when he reached sixty, Bower had sold his shares back to the firm at book value, a tradition that retiring partners have had to follow ever since.

In 1983, LEK broke away from Bain & Company. My partners and I were sued by Bain, perhaps to discourage other partners from leaving. I am very grateful to Bain for this: It made us feel that the equity in LEK was valuable (we had done nothing wrong, and after a few months we reached agreement with Bain's lawyers). When I "retired" from LEK after six years and sold my shares back to the other partners, I was able to argue that the equity should be valued on a market-related basis. Over a decade later, however, there is no sign that LEK is going to float.

At the height of the dot-com mania, many industry insiders thought that the pressure to float the "e-business" parts of firms like McKinsey and the Boston Consulting Group would be irresistible, and that consequently the whole practice would need to be floated to prevent internal defections to the e-business. The collapse in Internet stock market valuations came just in time to prevent this.

When a professional firm floats or sells itself, its current partners are really cashing in on both the past and the future. By coining in the goodwill and reputation of the firm's brand, built over many generations of partners, they are also shortchanging the future professionals. A consulting partnership is as near to a perfect meritocracy as is possible (which, in my experience, is still less than perfect).

If one particular firm, McKinsey, for example, does not go public, then future McKinsey partners will share the total future annual profits of the Firm. If the Firm does go public, it will have to declare earnings and dividends for its public owners; therefore, the partners will get less. They'll receive a nice income, but they will miss out on the profits on top. In every profession, advancement to the partnership is simply less attractive than it used to be.

When the partners of professional firms sell out, those in the next level down, the so-called "mezzanine layer," often will be hopping mad. Many defect to other firms and a few set up on their own, prompting some floating firms to provide a special deal for the mezzanine layer. Such efforts may not be enough, as a domino effect produces a ripple all the way down the professional chain. Ordinary consultants whose partners sell out are never happy.

Senior professionals in firms that don't float share in something larger than their own creation. The top people in the Boston Consulting Group not only make what they could make elsewhere—their sustainable income—they also benefit from the profits of the firm.

The profits derive, of course, from each year's work, but are not merely the result of the aggregate professional skill of the firm's members. The profits also derive from the firm's reputation and brand, which in older consulting firms will have been largely established before the current generation of partners took over. My friends at the top of BCG continue to benefit from Bruce Henderson's creation. My McKinsey friends are drawing on the "rent" that Marvin Bower put into the McKinsey name. While BCG and McKinsey partners cannot make a large fortune by selling out, they remain content to stay and make small fortunes each year.

When I talk to people at all levels of consulting firms, it becomes clear that the partnership model is both sustainable and attractive.

Barry: An 80/20 Partnership

Barry Jones, a senior vice president at the Boston Consulting Group and a former close colleague of mine, makes a telling point. "We are building a virtuous circle here," he comments. "I've been here for twenty-five years, and if you had told me that I would be with one firm for that long when I joined, I'd have said you were nuts. But, after twenty-five years, amazingly, I am still very happy here. It really feels like a family; it's a collegiate, fantastic organization.

"Yes, I do feel fairly rewarded. I could probably get more money outside, doing some job that I didn't really like, but money is not the be-all and end-all of life. For me, the combined financial and lifestyle package presented by BCG as a partnership is far more sustainable than a company on the stock exchange, or the deal-based culture of an investment bank. In neither would I feel that I am my own boss in the same way as at BCG.

"Over time, the firm and its brand become worth more and more. This gives a comfortable income to the vice presidents, and also acts as a magnet for our professional staff—not just the ones we have now, but also the ones we want in the future. By the time they become officers of the firm [partners], they and the current generation of officers will have made it even more valuable.

"Other human benefits," Jones continues, "are important, too. Socially, many of my friends are inside the firm. My colleagues' wives are friends with mine. Professionally, I enjoy the opportunity to spend time on things like developing the firm's intellectual capital—I'm currently head of its strategy practice. These are investments in the firm's library. You can't afford them if you are too interested in this year's profits and share price. At times, work in BCG is hard and the hours can be long, but I wouldn't say it's stressful. The partnership ethos is very real and colleagues support each other."

I asked Jones if BCG would ever sell out. "Emphatically, no. Because of the environment, we did look at it in the last two years but quickly dismissed it. If we sold the company we'd be betraying what we believe in and what makes BCG what it is. If someone wanted to propose that we sell, the rules are one partner, one vote, and a high acceptance hurdle. The younger partners want to work here for a lifetime—why would they sell out? And the older partners realize that what we enjoy today is purely a function of what was created in the past. More than 80 percent of us feel a real moral obligation to maintain the institution rather than make a quick buck that we don't need anyway."

The moral of Jones's story for 80/20 individuals is simply that the partnership model is an attractive one for individuals who are creating extraordinary value. The partnership model shares wealth fairly and helps build value for many generations of 80/20 individuals, without the need for the stock market or external investors. Keep in mind that the Boston Consulting Group did not start as a partnership. It bought itself out from its owners, the Boston Safe and Deposit Company, with its own cash flow. Perhaps your group of managers, if you are all 80/20 individuals adding much more wealth than you take, could propose a similar deal and begin a partnership.

Donna Dubinsky and Jeff Hawkins: An 80/20 Hybrid

The power of professionals within consulting or investment banking firms is matched by the actions of managers in conventional firms, so long as they know the value they provide. Jeff Hawkins and Donna Dubinsky demonstrated this when they invented the PalmPilot electronic personal organizer.

Turned away by venture capitalists who "knew" that handheld organizers were a surefire route to the poorhouse, in 1995 Hawkins and Dubinsky "settled" for $44 million from a corporation, U.S. Robotics.

Initially U.S. Robotics "let us run Palm independently . . . They were more like our bank than our boss," Dubinsky said later.[3] To the astonishment of the venture capitalists, PalmPilots became a huge cultural phenomenon and a financial success. Then the downside of the corporate coin emerged.

In 1996, U.S. Robotics was taken over by 3Com. 3Com tried to run PalmPilot as an integrated division. Hawkins and Dubinsky lost autonomy. They also lost money, as 3Com stock (the consideration they ended up with for selling PalmPilot) tanked.

Hawkins and Dubinsky entered a war of nerves with Eric Benhamou, the 3Com CEO. The inventors begged to spin PalmPilot off. No way, replied Benhamou. (By 1998, PalmPilot was the only bright spot in 3Com's world.) But Benhamou knew that Hawkins and Dubinsky held the better cards. They could always set up a competitor to PalmPilot.

Hawkins and Dubinsky did set up a new venture, Handspring, in 1999. Benhamou agreed to license the Palm operating system to them. He really had no choice. As Dubinsky said, "The alternative [for 3Com] was to push us into the arms of Palm operating system competitors or re-create a similar operating system ourselves. They knew it would be smarter to have us as their platform product partner."

What Dubinsky tactfully does not say is that Handspring's purpose was to create a cheaper and better alternative to the Palm line. As I write, it is executing this with great panache.

What do we make of this story?

- ❖ It is always a mistake to imprison 80/20 individuals in a corporate structure where they lack control and an ownership stake directly related to their venture. In the PalmPilot example, everyone suffered: Jeff, Donna, and the 3Com shareholders.
- ❖ No matter what deal or ownership structure is established, the value creators like Hawkins and Dubinsky hold the upper hand. Any value creator who is determined to capture the value that he or she creates can do so. A big corporation can buy an enterprise, products, and patents, but if the key people leave, so too does the growth.
- ❖ A "hybrid" deal between value creators and their corporations—like the one that Jeff and Donna eventually ended up with—is often best for everyone. But the value creators must have autonomy and an equity stake in their own venture.

What's the 80/20 Connection?

In addition to the two traditional routes for entrepreneurs—the management buyout and buyin, and starting an independent new venture—at least three hybrid structures are available, and may well be more attractive for some would-be entrepreneurs. The hybrids are basically individual-centered structures—run by 80/20 individuals—but they combine aspects of earlier corporate structures:

- ❖ In the partnership structure (the Barry Jones/BCG solution), partners buy the business from its owners using no external equity. The partnership structure is an ancient corporate form that adapts well to many fast-growth knowledge businesses, where the need for capital is low and the need to keep and attract moneymakers is high.
- ❖ In the host/profit-sharing solution, a new firm is set up

within another firm (Rick Haller's solution). The team maintains a contractual right to a share of the profits; the host company provides the capital and takes a share of annual profits as well. A similar solution can be applied to individual moneymakers like Richard, my investment banker friend. Another variant is a formal joint venture between a new team of entrepreneurs and an established corporation (which may be the one you work for now, or a third party).

❖ The incubator solution (which also used to be called corporate venturing) involves managers from one firm founding and taking a stake in a new venture (Jerry's solution). Whether or not there is an incubator, this model allows for widespread expansion. The bridge between the old firm and the new is sturdy and links between them remain in place.

How to Build Your 80/20 Business

Ask yourself three questions:

❖ Which solutions are potentially available to me? Do they make sense for the other parties involved (my partners, the managers and owners of the firm, or providers of capital)?
❖ Of the viable options, which structure will enable me to create something of greatest value?
❖ Which solution will make me happiest and most fulfilled?

1 Start a New Venture

Clearly, you could start a new venture. The downside is that you would have to leave your current business and its brands behind; you may also have to leave your customers, technology, and key colleagues. If you use capital from other people, especially if it comes from a venture capital institution, your new bosses may be more demanding than the old ones.

The upside is that the new business is yours. As long as you meet financial expectations, you can run it your own way. You will also keep much or most of the value you create.

The management buyout or buyin option depends on whether you have a willing seller, on the one hand, and whether you can make a good return for yourself and the capital provider on the other. The ideal profile for such a business is as follows:

❖ A low market value of the business, as reflected in a low price/earnings multiple (the total stock market value of the firm divided by its earnings). Very often public markets do not like small businesses in low-growth markets.

❖ High cash-generation potential. Cash flow is important so that the business can be leveraged using debt. A high proportion of debt means that less equity from venture capitalists is needed, which translates into a greater chance of meeting their high rate-of-return requirements—while still leaving money for you in the deal. A high interest charge also means that you will pay less tax.

❖ The potential to increase earnings (and the value of the company) when it is resold.

Management buyouts, especially by large quoted corporations, are a paradox. Private equity firms that initiate and finance the deals require a much higher rate of return than do shareholders on the stock exchange. How then can the firms outbid the shareholders to buy the companies?

The answer lies in three aspects of buyouts:

❖ They rely on undervaluation of the companies. The private equity people have to buy cheap. To some extent, buyouts are a conspiracy between the management and the private equity financiers to pay vendors less than the business is really worth.

❖ The buyout vehicle has superior leverage. Public companies do not like to load themselves up with debt, shareholders dislike it because it could interfere with the predictability of dividends, and managers avoid it because it pressures them to push the business forward. A buyout consists of as much or more debt than equity. But while this equity costs more than public money equity, the debt is much cheaper. The weighted average cost of capital can be lower in a buyout than on the stock exchange. (The risk, of course, is greater.) High leverage brings another benefit: a low rate of taxation. In the early years of a buyout, much of the operating profit pays off interest, resulting in a low tax charge.

❖ There is great motivation. In a buyout everyone is focused on achieving financial results; if they don't come, the consequences can be serious. In a typical corporation, especially one with several companies under its umbrella, the managers running any particular division are insulated from financial risk and cannot make their own decisions in response to market developments. Their motivation just isn't as intense as it ideally should be.

Buyouts are inherently stressful. Yet if the conditions are right, they are a great way to get rich.

I would never discourage a gung-ho 80/20 individual from pursuing a buyout or setting up his or her own new venture. These moves are good for business and society because they stimulate experimentation, they reduce the degree of "averaging" in the economy, they increase growth, and they help close the gap between the people who create wealth and those who receive it. I know many individuals whose lives have been transformed by a buyout's success or failure. Fortunately, the odds favor success.

If the buyout or new venture succeeds, nearly everyone's life is improved. The money alone may not lead to happiness, but financial independence offers you more choices and freedom to seek fulfillment.

Even if the business fails, you can still benefit. Use what you have learned to attempt a new venture or buyout in your current field or a new one. You may have lost money, but you've gained experience. Many 80/20 individuals who failed in their first venture or buyout went on to bigger and better things.

Yet, like Rachel, many 80/20 individuals want to avoid the hassle, risk, legal obligations, and loss of tribal support that go along with individual ownership.

By scaling down your capital needs, using your savings, and seeking backing from family, friends, and business angels, the pressures of starting a new venture can be reduced.

One often-ignored option may greatly benefit 80/20 individuals and society: Strike a deal with your employer or another company. The hybrid solutions—such as Jerry Bowskill's incubator deal, Rick Haller's team profit sharing, or Barry Jones' partnership—can work extremely well and involve less hassle, risk, obligation, and loss of tribal support.

2 Finding a Hybrid Solution

Hybrid solutions take you at least three-quarters of the way toward owning your own business, at half the normal mental and financial cost. A profit-sharing deal will save you from setting up a separate new legal entity. A partnership or incubator deal will allow you to keep the job and coworkers you love and respect. In every case, a new venture can emerge, featuring a reduced financial risk due to the corporate partner's complete or partial underwriting or provision of a semicaptive source of finance.

Hybrid solutions help established corporations by creating new value they would not have previously enjoyed.

They also benefit the economy and society because they usually lead to a chain of new ventures. Good ideas that might have never seen the light of day are liberated. Returns are "de-averaged," as those who create wealth take a larger share of it. Individuals have greater control over their work and their lives. Their success will encourage others to become 80/20 individuals.

The world of the 80/20 individual is much wider and less daunting than the traditional image of entrepreneurs implies. Many 80/20 individuals have made deals with their corporations and remained part of a tribe. Many more would be willing to capitalize on their wealth creation if they knew that such options existed. Now they do.

Nevertheless I must offer a word of caution. Don't confuse a hybrid 80/20 deal with an existing corporation with initiatives sent down from top management. Concepts like profit centers, "entrepreneurial units" within corporations, the "individualized corporation,"[4] "intrapreneur" programs, and the "empowerment" of individuals and teams are attempts to rejuvenate and energize existing corporations, not to encourage new ventures. Such initiatives are welcome; they are likely to help rather than harm. They could easily spill over into hybrid solutions that involve the creation of new businesses. But unless and until they do, no change in wealth has occurred. The corporation, not the individual, is still creating—and keeping—the wealth.

Three differences separate 80/20 deals from corporate makeovers. A genuine new venture

❖ is proposed by an individual or small team—*not* by the head honchos

❖ involves the transfer of real ownership, or a substantial slice of the profits, to 80/20 individuals

❖ leaves a new team free to run the business the way they want, as long as they respect certain property (brands, patents, or other shared property) that is still owned by the larger corporation

More succinctly, it is run by 80/20 individuals for 80/20 individuals.

When most of the value in a business belongs to the individual wealth-creators, as in Barry Jones's consulting company or Rick Haller's investment banking venture, then the team creating the value is strongly positioned to negotiate with its current owners or a new corporate partner. For example, the Boston Consulting Group bought itself out from the Boston Safe and Deposit Company and became a partnership, and Rick Haller's team created its own terms when dealing with banks.

In most branches of commerce, however, the relative contributions of the individual and small team compared to the total corporation are not so clear-cut. In fact, they are usually not worth arguing about—I am not advocating a form of small team trade unionism, where the team creating growth haggles with its employers to gain a share of the profits. The owners and board of the corporation will propose compensation based on their own interests. If this compensation fails to meet industry standards—if the top value creators leave—only then will the board understand its miscalculation.

Haggling for a pay raise or waiting for the board to compensate you isn't enough; 80/20 individuals take control of their own fate. If an individual's or small team's skills and ability to create wealth are not confined to their organization—as with Rick Haller and his team—they should negotiate an entrepreneurial deal with a third-party corporation. Haller's deal illustrates this is possible even when the corporate partner provides a necessary ingredient—in Haller's case, capital and banking status. This deal created wealth both for the 80/20 individuals and the third-party corporation. Even if the first bank had not agreed, Haller could have crossed the street to another one. Richard, the investment banker, did, and even as a one-person business, managed to keep most of his profits.

If the individual and small team want to start a business, but doubt the portability of their skills, they can still create a new venture by calling on those powerful business genes—the ideas that create wealth. Most of these ideas may seem suited solely to the team's current corporation, but with a little tweaking, could probably benefit the entire industry. Remember, no one really *owns* ideas.

Rachel: An 80/20 Case Study of a Manager

The powerful business genes that led to Rachel's success do not belong to her corporation. Her ideas—a design-led market segment, concession retailing in department stores, cutting design costs in anticipation that only 40 percent of clothes will be sold at full price, organizing her business to minimize capital—are powerful business genes that anyone could exploit.

But seasoned 80/20 individuals like Rachel and her team who have already experienced the power of the principle have certain advantages others don't. They know the people outside the corporation to approach in order to create wealth—the individual fabric designers, for example—and how to interact with them.

The parent corporation that owns Rachel's business sits uneasily in the middle of this wealth-creation system. It owns the business but neither the ideas nor the people who make the business possible. This trend is occurring throughout the business world: As the bargaining power of individuals and small teams increases, it eats into the power of large firms.

I joke with Rachel that she is only 80 percent of an 80/20 individual: "You're missing the vital 20 percent, the ownership that comes with adding value."

Despite their success, the business still does not belong to Rachel's team. I tell her she has three choices. She can continue to be an employee, creating wealth and hoping that the corporation notices and rewards her. She can follow the traditional entrepreneurial path that relies on venture capital: arrange a buyout of her division, for example, or start a new venture from scratch. Or she can pursue the hybrid route, by building an alliance with her existing corporation or a new one.

One way to accomplish the hybrid would be to deal with the board of her current corporation. But the board is there to look out for shareholders' interests; they will prevent her from walking off with the existing business—unless she buys it. A deal that would benefit both her team and her current firm would be to create a new business—one separate from her current business. She could propose taking a share of the new profits that she would create in the new venture. But first, she'd need to find other people to plug the holes that would be created when she and her team members left for the new business. The existing business would have to continue to make profits for its owners.

One potential idea might be to start a new catalog business—selling by mail order and the Internet. The new business would use some of the property of the existing one, like customer names and addresses, but would be a separate entity. Or she could take the business genes that work so well in the existing market and apply them to a new market—menswear, a nonclothing business, or a different location. Any new business that adds to the firm's existing profits will create a win/win—for her and the team, the board and the current company. She would share in profits that would not otherwise be created.

Because she's a true 80/20 individual, Rachel is capable of creating much more than she is. The world would only benefit from two businesses run by her, and she deserves a substantial stake in the new one.

Using the 80/20 Principle to Exploit Corporations from Within

Individuals and small teams are well positioned to use the 80/20 principle to exploit their corporations in a perfectly ethical way. The individuals should identify the few really powerful business genes responsible for most, if not all, of the firm's success. Small teams can form, comprised of the best users of these business genes, individuals who excel at using ideas that power profits. 80/20 individuals find new ways to exploit the ideas that brought their firm success, adding new twists to create distinctive and even more attractive ventures.

80/20 individuals can either follow the traditional roads to forming a new venture, or can cut their existing firm in on the deal. A hybrid solution—a joint venture between the existing firm and 80/20 individuals—can add profits to the old firm while also starting the 80/20 individual on a less risky, more satisfying road to riches. A joint venture may lead to a bigger business and a bigger fortune to boot!

CHAPTER 9

Exploit Other Firms

There breaks out an epidemic that, in all earlier epochs,
would have seemed an absurdity—the epidemic of
overproduction. . . . there is too much civilization, too much
means of subsistence, too much industry, too much commerce.
—*Karl Marx and Friedrich Engels*

Companies have grown so productive that their markets
can no longer absorb the de facto increases in capacity that
continual productivity improvement creates.
—*Larry Shulman of the Boston Consulting Group*

The 80/20 individual's privilege is to select only the most profitable activities within the most profitable parts of markets: ones
that enjoy the highest returns on capital and require the least management effort.

By isolating these specific markets, an 80/20 individual can serve
the customers of these parts of the market far better than anyone else.
The individual should be able to provide a much better product or
service than the competitors and still make high returns. They will improve whatever dimensions the customer values most, be it speed,
convenience, features, quality, design, or even price.

But what happens if the most profitable activities cannot be marketed and sold on their own? For example, we knew that the most
profitable part of Zoffany Hotels was bedrooms, and that we lost
money on food and beverage activity. Yet, needless to say, our customers want, and deserve, to be offered food and drink. We could not
provide only bedrooms.

We decided to subcontract the undesired work—running our restaurants—to someone else. You, too, should subcontract all but the most profitable parts of your business. Exploit other firms. Make them do all your heavy lifting.

Actions at the level of the individual venture or remodeled business unit affect the economy as a whole. The 80/20 principle shows that a minority of activities fall in the superprofitable pool, the place where 80/20 individuals swim. So who should run the rest of the economy, the majority of business activity?

Not 80/20 individuals.

The "grunt work" should fall to the same corporations that run the economy today. And while most revenues will go to the existing corporate sector, most profits won't. They will belong to 80/20 individuals.

We've learned to view the individual as the "little guy" at the mercy of the big battalions, twisting and turning to find a niche neglected by the big boys. But today, niches are not consolations; they are first prizes.

Why are older and larger firms willing to be used by 80/20 individuals, allowing us to profit so much?

Overproduction Arrives at Last

We're in the right place at the right time. Corporations have been so productive and capital is so plentiful that the result is a serious over-supply of the option to make almost every physical good you could imagine. As Larry Shulman, senior vice president of the Boston Consulting Group, says, "More than a decade of investments in information technology and capital-goods spending has finally paid off."[1]

Yet this productivity surge is also a trap for mature companies. Continual productivity gains create headaches if they run ahead of the increase in market demand. And they do. In oil, cars, silicon chips, steel, you name it, supply is at least a third greater than demand. Mature firms pile up cash, but the excess capacity creates a buyer's market and the ever-present threat of price deflation.

The cash itself is also a problem. In the old days, firms with too much cash would simply diversify. But today, the 80/20 principle is so well understood by investment analysts (if not by CEOs) that it blocks this route. Instead, Mr. Shulman suggests, companies use excess cash to buy similar companies, especially abroad. What looks like rational globalization is really a side effect of an overabundance of cash. But that is another story.[2]

80/20 Individuals Benefit from Overproduction

Overproduction benefits new companies; those without productive capacity or the need to acquire it; those with customers and the ability to subcontract all but the most profitable activities to other firms.

The "buyer's market" we're experiencing benefits consumers less than it does the "in-between" firms that sell to consumers or profitable business customers, and who outsource most of their work to industrial firms.

People say the Internet and excess capacity gives power to customers. But that is only three-quarters right. Individual consumers have benefited from deflation of prices. Yet the failure of consumer brands to crumble into the dust and the willingness of consumers to support the economy in good times and bad are testimony to the resilience of consumer goods suppliers. From what many commentators say about increasing consumer power, you would think that the profits of branded goods suppliers would have tumbled. They have not; their profits are generally flat or rising.

What consumer goods firms lose to consumers in lower prices, they gain from their suppliers by keeping down the cost of bought-in goods. The really big winners are industrial buyers.

In business-to-business transactions, those with demand are striking terrific bargains with the poor suckers stuck with supply. Small, high-growth firms that have increasing demand from customers but who lack the capacity to make things are triumphing. What was once a quandary for 80/20 individuals is now a godsend.

In many industries new capacity may not be required for many decades—or ever. A new enterprise needs working capital, but should not need to invest in capital goods as there is already a glut of infrastructure and frozen capital. There are too many factories, too many machines within them, too many warehouses, too much retail space, even too many laboratories for research and development.

There are also too many people. Rather than address the problem of overexpansion by closing facilities and firing people, managers in mature firms usually prefer to welcome incremental orders from anywhere, regardless of their profitability. By doing this, these managers put their corporate capital, their know-how, their employees, and their contacts—assets that probably took years of blood, sweat, and hard cash to build—at the disposal of savvy 80/20 individuals for a knockdown price.

Believe it or not, the conditions for growth (recessions notwithstanding) have never been higher. What has changed is the *nature* of growth. The days when growth required investment in productive capacity are over. Today growth requires new ideas, new inspiration, new business models, variants of existing successful models, and new and better services. The essence of growth used to be physical—now it is intellectual.

This trend is much to the benefit of 80/20 individuals. For the first time, new ventures do not need to create their own corporate infrastructure. You don't need your own factories, warehouses, trucks, shops, offices, or laboratories. You may not even need your own brands or access to customers. You can use the property of older and larger firms. You can rent it, or enter a revenue-sharing or royalty arrangement; in each case, you can avoid the need for capital.

You may also be able to buy surplus assets or brands—perhaps even a whole business—at a fraction of the original cost.

Sometimes you can exploit other firms in your line of business, even if you are a potential competitor. If a large and successful firm hasn't been able to make a business work, it will doubt that a start-up, or a remodeled business run by a separate group of managers, could do so.

Plymouth Gin: How to Be a Cuckoo

Cuckoos cannot be bothered to raise their young. Instead, they deposit cuckoo eggs in the nests of other species of birds. These unsuspecting parents feed and protect the baby cuckoos, who reward this generosity by kicking their "siblings" out of the nest, or by eating them.

80/20 individuals can learn a lot from a cuckoo.

The proof lies in Plymouth Gin. This business dates back to 1793; during the first half of the twentieth century, it was a leading brand in America, Europe, and what remained of the British Empire. Cocktail recipe books generally specify the use of Plymouth Gin for pink gin and many other cocktails. The company that owned Plymouth Gin enjoyed a monopoly: While "London dry gin" can be made anywhere in the world, Plymouth Gin can be made only in Plymouth, England.

During the 1980s, control of Plymouth Gin fell to Whitbread, then to Allied Lyons, whose drinks portfolio included another premium gin, Beefeater. Rather than run two competing top brands, Allied decided to sideline Plymouth Gin.

By 1996, sales of Plymouth Gin were negligible. But a large working distillery still existed, with the capacity to produce huge volumes of gin. Rather than pay to close it down, Allied Domecq (as it had become) sold the company, brand, and distillery to my partners and me at a knockdown price.

Five years later the gin world was a different place. In the British premium gin market, Plymouth had overtaken Beefeater. But although the British drink a great deal of gin, the UK market comprises less than 10 percent of the world total. As Plymouth Gin's resurgence was confined to Britain, it barely dented the business of Beefeater, Tanqueray, or Bombay Sapphire.

However, in 2000, in a bid to internationalize, Plymouth Gin entered a strategic alliance with Vin & Sprit, the Swedish corporation that owns Absolut Vodka. We sold 50 percent of Plymouth Gin to Vin & Sprit, made a substantial profit, and gained access to Absolut's global distribution network. In 2001, Vin & Sprit entered joint ventures with both Jim Beam and Maxxium, ensuring that Plymouth Gin could be effectively marketed and sold throughout the world.

What had happened? My partners and I had started a remodeled management venture by using excess capital to buy a 203-year-old brand and a large distillery from a mature industry leader. (A remodeled management venture involves taking over an existing business and making it a separate new venture. Any group of managers can do this by offering to buy their division.) Because of perceived excess capacity, a well-run conglomerate giant was willing to unload this business—a liability or a fabulous heritage, depending on your viewpoint—for a tiny sum.

My partners, John Murphy and Charles Rolls, then built up the business in the United Kingdom so that it became sufficiently credible to interest another drinks industry leader. By striking a deal with Vin & Sprit, we then acquired the muscle to restore Plymouth Gin to its previous role as one of the world's leading premium gins, an enormously valuable position. If this potential is realized, Allied Domecq—owner of the Beefeater brand and the company that got us started—will surely rue the day that it sold its apparently defunct brand and distiller.

Nothing that we did could have happened without the two big, established companies who helped us. Yet they were more than willing to do so. Which mature industry giants are going to help you make a killing?

The Most Profitable Exploitation in the World

Back in the 1980s an 80/20 individual named Bill was running a very small computer company, making very small profits. But he didn't know which brand of software was going to outlast the other. So he created different teams for each system—DOS, OS/2, SCO Unix, Mac applications, and his firm's own developments. It seemed unlikely that any of the latter would win against older and better-funded rivals.[3]

Then Bill did something extremely clever. He parlayed his small company into an alliance with IBM, then at the height of its fortune. Bill's company agreed to develop software for the IBM personal computer (PC), with no restriction on the use of that software for other computers. The decision to use "open architecture" helped IBM achieve extraordinary growth in its sales of PCs. It was not, however, profitable growth. The attractive activity—the one that generated few sales but many profits—lay in the operating system software. Bill's alliance with IBM settled the issue; that one move set Bill Gates on a course that would make him the planet's richest person.

Hindsight is, of course, a wonderful thing. It is easy to say that IBM should have realized Microsoft had far more to gain than IBM from an alliance. But IBM focused on its own agenda, rather than that of its partners. If it had insisted on buying a large share in Microsoft as a condition of the alliance, Gates could not have refused. But IBM didn't insist, perhaps because Microsoft was too small a corporation for such a stupendously successful company to bother with.[4]

Microsoft's story is atypical only in the scale of the consequences. Time and time again—as the Allied Domecq sale of Plymouth Gin to 80/20 individuals also shows—large, mature companies' deals with small ventures greatly favor the "little guy." Large, established companies seem to have a knack for being exploited by small, new ones.

Rachel: An 80/20 Case Study of a Manager

Rachel uses other firms for a majority of the product and service that her firm provides. Design is executed by individual designers and small outside firms. Manufacturing is also done by third parties. Department store sales are made by Rachel's people, even though the stores are owned and operated by other firms. Rachel has limited her operations to the conception and orchestration of her system and to direct contact with customers.

Rachel could have done this for herself with her own firm. The only important thing her employer "gave" her was a respected brand. Yet, as the Plymouth Gin experience shows, it might have been possible for her to acquire and build on a dying brand. The brand might not have been necessary—she has built three others from scratch.

Rachel agrees: "What I needed at the time from my company was the security and confidence that came from being part of a big company. Yet I knew even then it was best not to rely on [that company's] resources or its ways of doing things. I knew I had to build a small team of people and that we had to rely on ourselves and on deals we could strike with outside firms. I suppose we were exploiting other firms."

The Pursuit of Growth

Overcapacity is not the only reason for large, mature companies to seek alliances with younger and smaller ones. The other main reason is lack of growth.

If we exclude acquisitions, almost no *Fortune* 50 company has ever grown at more than 5 percent per annum.[5] It appears that size and growth are incompatible, which explains why large firms are often eager to enter strategic alliances with smaller ventures.

In the early days of LEK Consulting, when we were short on clients, we entered into an alliance with PA Consulting, a large, established firm. The deal was simple. Members of PA's network provided leads and introduced us to clients. When we became part of the family, PA clients were more inclined to use us. In return we gave PA half the profits we earned and a new high-growth product line.

It worked reasonably well. Although PA "gave" us only a few clients, they were large, long-standing, and profitable engagements, which, as I explained before, are the best kind. But over time, LEK, which retained its own brand, became stronger and less dependent on PA. As we were growing rapidly, the constraint on growth became internal—affecting our ability to coach and train good professional staff—rather than external. After a while, the aid PA provided was hardly worth the cost. When we ended the relationship with PA, we kept all of "its" clients.

The moral of the story is to make open-ended deals with larger corporations, ones that allow you to compare their contribution to their take. In general, the new venture will gain more in the beginning than it will over time. For this reason the corporation will probably try to negotiate an equity stake in the venture. But 80/20 individuals should insist on a deal based on a share of revenues or profits that can be easily terminated.

Alliances are useful but they needn't be permanent. Get engaged but not married.

How to Exploit Other Firms

1 Identify Missing Ingredients in Missing Markets

While thinking about which new business or idea to launch, reflect on the large companies you know, and think about the missing ingredients that have eluded them. Mature companies often possess nine-tenths of the puzzle: They have brands, manufacturing assets, and access to markets, but they lack the imagination to generate growth. If you can find the small missing piece of the jigsaw, you'll be made.

When economists talk about "missing markets," they're referring to the existence of recognizable opportunities that no one has capitalized on.[6] Only individuals can do this.

Individuals have local knowledge. However, individuals rarely do anything with their knowledge. As the great Austrian economist F. A. Hayek explained in 1945, because local knowledge is not exploited fully, the economy does not grow as fast as it could:

> The peculiar character of the problem of a national economic order is . . . that the knowledge of the circumstances of which we must make use never exists in concentrated or integrated form, but solely as the dispersed bits of incomplete and frequently contradictory knowledge which all the separate individuals possess. The economic problem of society is . . . how to secure the best use of resources known to any of the members of society . . . it is a problem of the utilization of knowledge not given to anyone in its totality.[7]

It is up to you to add your local knowledge to the raw materials of business that already exist in large, mature corporations.

In the case of Plymouth Gin, my partners knew how to revive a defunct brand. Whether the brand managers within Allied Domecq had these skills or not, they failed to use them. There was a missing market until my partners added the secret ingredient.

The second and third hotels acquired by Zoffany Hotels came from a respected hotel chain, Trust House Forte. It sold them cheaply because it could not make them work. Trust House Forte operated around a central reservation system for bookings, but lacked demand in small towns with no tourist trade. The missing ingredient here was simple: local marketing of the hotel to business users. But Zoffany stepped in with managers trained to scour the local community for business. Measured by return on sales and return on capital, these hotels are now two of the most profitable in England.

Think how much more attractive it would be for you to take a ready-made solution from existing corporations than to start something from scratch. You don't need to invent a new recipe; simply borrow one!

Try this exercise: On the left side of a blank sheet of paper write down all the large organizations you know well. In the middle, identify their missing markets: businesses they could have but don't, or businesses they do have that are not profitable. On the right, identify each missing ingredient. If the missing ingredient is something you have or could appropriate from elsewhere—maybe by inviting a new partner into your consortium—then you have discovered a ready-made new venture.

If this fails to trigger a new business idea, pull out a second sheet of paper. Write down all the ingredients—unusual insights, skills, or assets—that you and your team possess. Then look for an existing firm, or several, that have the raw material for a new venture but lack these ingredients. The ingredients supplied by the other firm or firms must make up a majority of the activity in the new venture, but your ingredient alone must make it viable and highly profitable.

When you have a shortlist of such firms, approach them to see if they will provide the materials you need, either by renting them to you (under a royalty or revenue-sharing arrangement), selling them, or entering a joint venture (a share profits or equity deal) with you. Generally it is better to rent than to buy, because this lowers risk and preserves capital, and better to buy than to joint venture, because the latter involves sacrificing a share of profits.

When you approach the other firm, establish how you can help; position your proposition in terms of how they will benefit. There is no need to point out that they will help your fledgling business many times more than you will help them.

2 Adhere Strictly to the 80/20 Frugality Principle

The 80/20 frugality principle (based on my own observations, not Pareto's original law) says: Undertake only those activities that yield a very high return on your capital and efforts.

If a task has a low return, you should not perform it. But if your customers insist on a bundled purchase, outsource that task to another company.

Even if a division appears to be very profitable, it still may be better to outsource the work if it absorbs energy that could be better used to generate even higher profits.

To outperform your competitors you'll need to provide some unique products or services to your customers. Often, though, businesses do too much and engage other firms to do too little. Remember that it is more difficult to stop doing something than it is to avoid it in the first place.

The two best "choke points"—areas that prevent excess work on your part—are capital and labor. Scrutinize every point where capital or employees will be used. Ask yourself whether it would be better to use another firm's capital or labor. Only if the work concerned is highly profitable (20 percent use of your efforts resulting in 80 percent of your rewards) or if no lower-cost alternative exists should you agree to use your own capital or employees.

New ventures once typically required more capital and more people than originally planned. Now whenever I look at a business plan, I reduce the amount of capital and the number of employees to 25 percent of the original level proposed without reducing revenues or profits. By winnowing your business down to the necessary dimensions you let other companies do the bulk of the work for you.

3 Separate Drones from Star Partners, Temporary from Permanent Deals

There are two types of transactions with third parties: the one-time deal, like buying Plymouth Gin from Allied Domecq, and the permanent deal, like the 50/50 venture between Plymouth Gin and Vin & Sprit.

For one-time deals the quality of the partner does not matter. The bargain ends as soon as it begins.

Resist permanent alliances initially. It's better to start with looser deals from which you can easily escape. Do not sell equity unless you have to, or unless the other party can very clearly add long-term benefits.

In permanent alliances the quality of the partner is vital. Expect a skewed distribution: fewer than 20 percent of possible partners are likely to provide 80 percent of the possible value to you.

Whenever possible when entering a permanent alliance, ensure that you can select the partner firm. Otherwise, how can you be sufficiently selective? If you are approached by another firm proposing a joint venture, make an exhaustive list of all possible substitute firms. One will probably be much better.

Clearly an intermediate area exists where a deal may last for a fixed period and be renewable by mutual consent. If you intend the deal to last forever, behave as if it will.

4 Force Birds of a Different Feather Together

Growth ultimately derives from individuals, in other firms as well as in your own. As always, a large majority of growth or potential growth—for which you and your team are the catalyst—will derive from a few of the individuals in the firm or firms with which you collaborate.

Finding these individuals is hard but worth it. Once you identify them, you'll have to motivate them. Don't assume that they share your obsession with profits.

As my business partner says: "In dealing with the managers inside [another firm], when we started, we went about it the wrong way. We thought that they would be turned on by the profit opportunity. Then we realized that what they liked more was top-line growth. In fact, we discovered, it wasn't really the financial side at all. They liked being part of a growth project. They had seen and enjoyed being part of an earlier megagrowth story, and they wanted to do the same thing again. They liked the excitement, the advertising campaigns, the glitz, and the momentum. It was as simple as that."

If the managers in other firms are not that interested in profits, you're free to use other, cheaper, ways to motivate them. Identify their "hot buttons." Perhaps all they want is a new challenge and a sense of shared achievement. It is important that the individuals you work with like you and see your project as theirs as well.

Individuals have different insights and access to different resources. Birds of a feather flock together, yet business opportunity comes when birds of a different feather cross paths.

Attaining local knowledge requires an understanding of the "power of weak ties," places where a large number of infrequent and shallow relationships between disconnected groups is more valuable than connections between similar groups.[8]

Add the insight from the 80/20 principle—that in any combination of relationships among individuals, a select few of them will contain most of the value—and you have a potent brew for innovation. Before you start your venture, look far and wide for individuals whose local knowledge differs from yours, yet whose style complements yours. Delay your launch until you have found a match made in heaven.

What 80/20 Individuals Can Do

Large and mature companies driven by excess capacity and by the realization that growth is easier across rather than within their corporate boundaries are more willing than ever to do business with 80/20 individuals.

80/20 individuals are in a prime position to establish successful new ventures because they

❖ Are ultraselective in the activities they undertake—they stick to what is superprofitable and supersimple

❖ Use other companies to do most of their work
❖ Provide the "missing link" to unlock huge hidden value
❖ Establish ties with the right companies
❖ Search out within these companies the right individuals with the right chemistry, at the right time, who embody the right mix of different local knowledge.

CHAPTER 10

Secure Capital

It's true we don't have much money so what we have to do is think.
—*Professor Ernest Rutherford, the man who split the atom*

80/20 individuals have always exploited capital. They have been the few who started with little capital—usually not their own—and ended with a cornucopia of cash. All businesspeople—whether managers, self-employed, or entrepreneurs—use capital. 80/20 individuals in each of these roles share the ability to get an extraordinary return on the capital they use.

Christopher: An 80/20 Case Study in High Returns

Raising starting capital has never been easy. The patron saint of 80/20 individuals is Christopher Columbus (1451–1506), the person in history who created the most value with the least capital.

Columbus was convinced that three small ships were all he needed to discover a westward route to the Indies. But he spent much longer trying to raise the money than on the voyage itself.

Being an Italian, he tried to raise money from Italian princes. He had his choice of sponsors since Italy had dozens of separate kingdoms and courts. Accordingly, he traipsed across Italy, outlining his plans to King This and Count That. They all thought his project was stupid.

He then became a subject to the duke of Anjou in France. Capital requisition refused again.

He switched his allegiance to the king of Portugal. Another rejection slip.

He presented his plan to the duke of Medina-Sedonia. No dice.

Next he tried the count of Medina-Celi. A crazy scheme.

Then the king and queen of Spain, who also said no, but more politely.

Not one to give up easily, Columbus finally saw a turn in luck when in 1492 he witnessed the fall of Granada, the Moors' stronghold, to the Spanish forces. Realizing that Queen Isabella would be in a good mood, he tried again. Success at last! Ten weeks after setting sail, Columbus kissed the ground he "discovered" and named it San Salvador.[1]

Three Lessons Handed Down from Columbus

1. If your project will change the world and have a very high return on capital, don't take "no" for an answer.

2. A less obvious but equally valuable message is that capital is not really a commodity and never has been. You raise "capital," but capitalists do not really exist. You raise money from individuals (who happen to have capital). But it is the individuals' support you use—and each person has different criteria and attitudes toward his or her investments.

3. Capital itself obeys the 80/20 principle. A select few uses of capital will be extraordinarily productive. Capital is always lying about idle or under-exploited. Columbus's project required a tiny fraction of the wealth available in hundreds of European courts of the time. What created massive wealth for Columbus, for Spain, and for the world was one person's idea and one person's commitment to make it happen, not the availability of capital.

A tiny minority of capital creates a large majority of wealth. The multiplying factors are the idea and 80/20 individuals. For two centuries Spain lived off its investment in Columbus's ships. Any two-bit count willing to take a chance could have chosen to back Columbus, incidentally changing the course of history (Spain would never have been so wealthy or important, and the count's province would have become a Great Power).

A Few Big Hits Create Wealth for Society

Before modern times the world's stock of wealth stagnated. Annual economic growth was close to zero, because wealth was applied to pursuits that didn't have any net economic payoff to society: It all went to conspicuous consumption by the state and the aristocracy, to war or religion (often the same thing, as in the Crusades), to lawsuits, or to building castles or wonderful gardens. Most of these projects were wasteful: Though some were of priceless aesthetic value to posterity, none made the economy grow. Wealth changed hands but did not accumulate.

The economy began to grow from the fourteenth century on, when a minority of wealth was applied to trade and technology and hence to the development of industry. Projects like Columbus's and those of other traders consumed a small proportion of Europe's available capital, yet led to nearly all economic growth. The returns on these successful projects were enormous.

When the economy grows at 2 percent a year, not every business or household experiences a 2 percent growth rate. Some businesses will have shrunk; others will have grown at 20 percent, 50 percent, or even 100 percent. Most growth comes from a minority of businesses that are growing very fast. The businesses themselves contain many products and projects, most with low or negative growth, but a few whose profits are mushrooming. When we analyze the averages, we find that just a few points of extreme growth contribute to most of society's overall growth rate.

Capital is the same. Some projects have returns in the hundreds or thousands of percents. Most have low or negative returns. Wealth accumulates through the very few productive projects, and by allocating more capital to the most productive users: 80/20 individuals.

Capital Is Now Less of a Barrier to 80/20 Individuals

Although today's financiers are sometimes as blind as the duke of An-jou, and the count of Medina-Celi, I have qualified good news for 80/20 individuals.

It is now easier to get capital than ever before, and more is being allocated to new enterprise. Also, nowadays less capital is needed to successfully launch a business of any size or profit potential.

Under the Roman Empire the economy was not organized in a way that rewarded investment in technological projects. The Roman Empire, like nearly all premodern societies, rewarded military, political, and agricultural prowess, and, in its declining years, skill in advancing religion.

The essence of modern capitalism is not the existence and proliferation of capital, but its application to trade, technology, and business in general. And a small amount of capital can have a relatively great effect.

Throughout history, 20 percent of capital has always produced more than 80 percent of cash returns—when the capital concerned is applied to high-return business projects. However, with the absolute level of investment in business ventures higher than ever, so too is global growth.

Productivity growth has become less dependent on large amounts of capital. For centuries, growth in the economy required heavy investment, and investment required capital. In the mid-nineteenth century, Karl Marx invented capitalism—the economy revolved around capital.

From about 1850 to 1970, in every country—capitalist, socialist, or communist—the importance of capital grew, yet things grew tougher for the individual entrepreneur. In this age of the large public company, the large organization, capital was the scarce resource, and capital accumulated within large corporations.

Funding any particular big business corporation was beyond the means of the individual and his family. While most business activity in the nineteenth century took place in medium-sized, national, family-financed and family-run enterprises; in the twentieth century, most business was transacted through large, multinational, publicly financed corporations run by managers who were not owners. The entrepreneur was less important than the manager; the individual less important than the corporation.

Many astute and sympathetic observers thought that the entrepreneur was doomed. The great economist Joseph Schumpeter, writing in 1942, penned an elegy for the entrepreneur:

> *The essential point to grasp is that in dealing with capitalism we are dealing with an evolutionary process. . . . a fundamental change is upon the capitalist process. . . .*
>
> *The social function [of the entrepreneur] is already losing importance and is bound to lose it at an accelerating rate . . . innovation itself is being reduced to routine. Technological progress is increasingly becoming the business of trained specialists who turn out what is required and make it work in predictable ways. The romance of early commercial enterprise is rapidly wearing away. . . .*
>
> *The perfectly bureaucratized giant industrial unit not only ousts the small or medium-sized firm and "expropriates" its owners, but also the entrepreneur . . . and the bourgeoisie as a class . . . stands to lose not only its income but also what is infinitely more important, its function.[2]*

So the barrier to the twentieth-century entrepreneur was capital and its increasing concentration in large corporations. However, capitalism has evolved yet again, beyond the stage where "capitalism" is a useful description. (Those who, like me, support free enterprise, should be willing to give up Marx's anachronistic label.) The increasing power of the 80/20 principle means that capital has become detached from its previous association with large-scale corporations.

The Link between Capital Investments and Growth Has Been Smashed

Individual capital providers and 80/20 individuals have aligned to produce higher returns than those available in conventional, publicly listed corporations. Capitalists have looked for the few investments that have the highest returns. The proof is the large-scale emergence, since 1970, of venture capital and private equity. Although a minority of capital is still devoted to private rather than public equity, private equity has enjoyed much higher returns.

Growth used to be related to physical materials. New companies set up camp near their sources of raw material, or power for their machines. Until the last thirty years people assumed that growth in the economy required a similar growth in physical goods and hence in capital. As a young management consultant in the late 1970s, I recall wading through masses of import and export statistics, which were always listed both in value and in weight.

But today no one cares about the weight of trade. Federal Reserve Board Chairman Alan Greenspan estimates that the weight of U.S. GDP today is about the same as in 1900, although its value has multiplied 20 times.

Physical objects and heavy industry are capital-intensive. Light industry is less so, and services hardly at all. And for each dollar of sales, 20 percent less capital is needed than twenty-five years ago. As a result, about $530 billion less capital is needed.

The 80/20 principle has smashed the link between capital investment and economic growth. Between 1994 and 2000, U.S. productivity grew by 2.8 percent a year, much higher than usual. Over half of the growth came from information technology (IT), which is not capital intensive. The capital stock of IT is less than 1 percent of total U.S. capital stock. This is a greater than 50/1 relationship, an extreme form of the 80/20 principle.

Growth in today's economy is not greatly driven by capital, but by technology, ideas, and 80/20 individuals. Technology has freed itself from capital. Economist Lester Thurow avows, "Without his furnace, Bessemer could not have made steel."[3] 80/20 individuals no longer need such expensive tools.

The terms of trade between capital and entrepreneur have swung in our favor. Yet everyone still overestimates the value of capital and underestimates really powerful ideas and 80/20 individuals.

What generates wealth today is not capital, but a small nucleus of capital coated with a larger outer ring of powerful ideas and initiative fueled by individuals. Not capital, but capital plus: capital + ideas; capital + 80/20 individuals.

Two Reasons for Caution

First, while it's easier than ever before to raise capital, it is still difficult. Having sat on both sides of the funding fence over the past dozen years, I've learned that the capital provider has more power than the idea generator.

Second, 80/20 individuals nearly always need some capital, usually more than they expect!

Most new firms go bust, always because they run out of cash. The most difficult time to raise money is not at the start. It's when you've been funded, but have run out of cash.

How to Use Capital

1 Use Capital Only When You Can Multiply It

Whether you are a manager or an entrepreneur, each unit of capital you use should triple within a few years. Twenty percent of capital produces 80 percent of returns. Eighty percent of capital produces 20 percent of returns. You don't want any of your capital to be in this latter 80 percent.

Will you multiply capital? Study your business plan and estimate what the total return to capital should be. For example, if you raise $1 million of capital, will you be able to return at least $3 million of capital when the business is sold?

This is the "cash-to-cash" ratio used by venture capitalists. They like to see a cash-to-cash ratio of at least three times, but prefer five, ten, or even more.

The other test that venture capitalists apply is the "internal rate of return" or IRR. This daunting phrase simply means the average compound percentage return to capital over time. For example, if you use

$1 million of capital and it takes one year to turn it into $3 million, this would be an IRR of 200 percent (the profit would be $2 million, twice the starting stake). If it takes three years to turn $1 million into $3 million, the IRR would be 44 percent.

You'll need a calculator to determine the IRR, but you can check it by multiplying as follows:

Year 1 $1.00m × 1.44 = $1.44m
Year 2 $1.44m × 1.44 = $2.07m
Year 3 $2.07m × 1.44 = $3.00m

For a new business, a venture capitalist may require a 50 percent IRR. You can work out the total return needed each year to justify this venture:

Year 1 $1.00m × 1.5 = $1.5m
Year 2 $1.50m × 1.5 = $2.25m
Year 3 $2.25m × 1.5 = $3.38m
Year 4 $3.38m × 1.5 = $5.06m

and so on.

The total return on your new business plan may be unsatisfactory. It may reveal over three years a cash-to-cash ratio of two times, which translates into an IRR of only 26 percent. Divide your business as many different ways as you can: by product, by channel, by customer or customer type, by geography, by technology used. Examine the return on capital—the cash-to-cash and IRR ratios—for each split.

For example, if you find that the return over the three-year period is as follows:

Product A uses $0.5 of capital and returns $0.75m
Product B uses $0.25 of capital and returns $1.5m
Product C uses $0.25 of capital and returns -$01.25m

The ratios for the three products are therefore:

	Cash-to-Cash Ratio	Internal Rate of Return
Product A	1.5 times	14%
Product B	6 times	82%
Product C	0.25 times	Negative
Total/average	2 times	26%

You would clearly decide to forget about Products A and C, and build a business around Product B. Or, if you are working within an organization, these calculations can be used to decide which new product to launch, or which business to expand or jettison.

Always analyze the returns for each lump of capital used. A tighter focus will make you richer.

2 Reduce Your Need for Capital

Reducing the need for capital does not mean reducing the size or upside of your new venture. The way to reduce your need for capital is to get it from other firms. Limit your activities, not your ambitions.

For every dollar of cost you have, you should normally have two or more dollars of external cost; in other words, at least two-thirds of your costs should be bought-in goods and services. This way, the majority of "real" capital you use will never figure in your books. Export at least two-thirds of your capital need, preferably three-quarters.

3 Raise More Capital than You Need

If capital is so expensive, is this dumb? Nope.

One percent of capital can lead to 99 or 100 percent of damage. If that 1 percent is the capital you don't have, it will force you under.

Since new ventures are inherently unpredictable, don't trust your plan entirely. Cut the amount of capital you need through structural policy decisions, tight focus, and outsourcing. Then allow yourself a very generous margin of error in estimating your need for capital. Raise $1.5 million of capital for every $1 million you think you need.

4 Provide Your Own Capital

The proof that capital is not a commodity is that its price varies enormously. Twenty percent of capital will constitute more than 80 percent of the cost. 80/20 individuals think very hard about where to get capital and what it costs.

I've ranked the main sources of capital from cheapest to most expensive:

- Capital made unnecessary by other firms (outsourcing)
- Suppliers and other creditors, and billing customers in advance (negative working capital)
- Your own savings
- Capital from family and friends
- Bank debt
- Capital from your existing employer
- Capital from alliances with other firms
- Public equity (from floating on the stock market)
- Angel equity (from rich individuals)
- Specialist industry sources of finance (e.g., insurance companies)
- Private equity (for developing businesses)
- Venture capital (for new businesses)

Near the top of the list are your own savings. Make it an iron rule to save 10–20 percent of your income. It won't be easy, and you may have to live without certain luxuries, but it is always possible to save 10–20 percent if you have it automatically deducted when you are paid.

5 Use the Cheapest Available Sources of External Capital

Use other firms' capital by outsourcing, and seek capital from suppliers and other creditors. Use customers' money by charging them in advance; sympathetic clients are surprisingly willing to do this for a new business, while consumers often expect to pay for a service in advance (examples include subscriptions or service contracts). When I was a management consultant, we changed the rules by asking for fees before we undertook the work; we were rarely refused.

Capital from family and friends will generally be cheaper and less onerous than capital from third parties. Friends and family are more likely to be able to help than they were a generation ago. Long business cycles and higher stock markets have put spare cash into many more pockets.

Bank debt may also be quite cheap, generally 1–3 percent above bank rates, although you often have to give the security of your assets, probably your house. If the business fails and you lose your home, such a loan may turn out to be horribly expensive. If at all possible— and it often is—secure bank debt on the assets of the business you are buying, not on your personal possessions.

A joint venture with your existing employer will be particularly tempting if the firm is willing to provide the new capital required. "Internal" capital, from the employer, is much cheaper than external capital. With luck, your new venture's funds will be costed only slightly above the old firm's required rate of return (despite the much higher risk). If the internal money is cheap, it is worth taking significantly more than you think you need.

When negotiating with an existing employer, insist that you and your team receive a chunky proportion of the equity: at least one-third for the team if the firm is providing all the cash, and more if the team is providing some cash. Also, try to cap the firm's return—when a certain level of return (value of the business when you sell it) is met, ask that 100 percent of the extra benefit goes to the team. You may have to settle for a lower number, but it is reasonable to argue that the team should receive a disproportionate share of any megaprofits; this bonus is known to venture capitalists as a "ratchet," because beyond a certain success condition, the team's share ratchets up to a higher percentage.

Consider funding from "business angels," rich individuals. You are likely to secure a much better deal from individuals than from venture capital or private equity institutions.

Specialist industry finance is another attractive option. For example, hotel companies looking to expand once had only three sources of funds: bank debt, public equity, and private equity. Now there is another opportunity: a deal with insurance companies or pension funds who fund hotel acquisitions in exchange for a fixed long-term rental.

Even within the venture capital and private equity community, shop around for the best possible deal. Different houses have different views on particular industries, technologies, types of business, and management teams. Venture capital and private equity will always be expensive, but there can be staggering differences between deals offered on the same transaction.

Never confine yourself to one potential funder, even if you are offered a reasonable deal. Go to three or four other companies and comparison-shop. Even when you are close to a deal, keep another horse in the race right to the end. This is not only wise insurance; it also ensures that you don't get screwed at the last minute. Play one source of capital against another to improve your terms.

When you negotiate with venture capital professionals, remember they have experience as well as cash on their side. You will raise money only once or a few times; they assess deals every day. Even up the odds by hiring an experienced lawyer or corporate financier who is willing to help in the nitty-gritty deal-making.

6 Be Obsessed with Cash

Any business venture is like Monopoly or any other cash-driven board game. You start with a small amount of cash, with the goal of turning it into a large amount of cash. Your ability to do this is the best test of whether you are adding economic value. An obsession with cash is the acid test of 80/20 individuals, who create unusually high value by adding a small amount of cash to extraordinarily powerful ideas.

Each year, examine the relationship between capital used and cash returned for any product, activity, customer, distribution channel, and region you work with. Look for the vital few cases where returns are inordinately high. Move heaven and earth to expand this business. Raise the returns on the rest or stop allocating capital to them.

7 Treat Capital Providers as Valued Partners

Capital is not a commodity, nor are its providers. The 80/20 principle applies to capital providers, too: Some are much more successful than others.

Choose successful capital providers. If they criticize your plan, there is probably something wrong with it. In my experience, successful capital providers have intuitive skills that even they undervalue. A suggested tweak to your ideas, a throwaway line here, a tentative hint there—all can be very helpful.

Treat your capital providers as full partners. Take your obligations seriously. Exceed every budget, target, and expectation. If you cannot do this, be open and honest. If you suspect things are going wrong, let them know sooner rather than later. If your fears are groundless, you will have gained a reputation for prudence; if things prove dicey, the unpleasant surprise will be less sudden and resonant.

In a way, capital providers act as the economy's conscience for your venture. The goal of the 80/20 individual who catches on to the coattails of powerful business genes should be to multiply capital. If things go wrong, either the business genes are less powerful than you thought, or you are tied less securely to their coattails than your rivals. The economy will only tell you whether you are succeeding or not, whether you are multiplying cash. The capital providers can help you work out why.

Keeping Score

Ideas and 80/20 individuals drive business progress. Capital keeps the score. There is no such thing as a good business that cannot multiply capital. 80/20 individuals start with a very small amount of capital and end up pumping out masses of the stuff.

The paradox of the 80/20 principle is that if capital became too cheap, it would cease to perform its function.[4] 80/20 individuals leverage and exploit capital, but also respect its scarcity. High capital cost is the best spur to extraordinary performance. Once you feel that capital is abundant, leave the company and start again. Your job in that particular business is done.

We should be eternally grateful to venture capitalists, both for making capital available and for keeping its price so high. As a result, 80/20 individuals can always find a way to make extraordinary returns on capital.

CHAPTER 11

Make Zigzag Progress

Failure or success seem to have been allocated to men by their stars. But they retain the power of wriggling . . . and in the whole universe the only really interesting movement is this wriggle.

—*E. M. Forster*

Using Innovation to Reach the Second Stage of Growth

An 80/20 individual's biggest challenge is not conceiving the business idea, assembling the team, raising the money, or even getting the business off the ground. It occurs once the idea is successful. Short of selling a business or product line off immediately, how do you develop the business creatively so that it can fulfill its potential?

The answer is the difference between making a good return—perhaps multiplying the capital by 5 to 10 times—and making a return in the 10- to 1,000-times range.

A venture or management unit that can make a 5-times return within, say, four years, should be capable of making a 25-times return within eight years. Over both periods the internal rate of return is about 50 percent.

But the difference in what 80/20 individuals pocket can be enormous. Because of ratchets, a creative individual may walk away with $5 million after four years, but $50 million after eight years.

Of course, it's not all about money. 80/20 individuals who have successfully launched a terrific new idea, product, or service want to see it flourish in every way. They want to see their colleagues—including new, younger recruits—grow and get rich. They don't want to be a flash in the pan. They want their reputations to rest on a permanently successful addition to their company and the economy.

The more successful an enterprise is in its first three to five years, the greater the upside for the future—if it can maintain its upward trajectory.

There's the rub. It is not easy to keep a brilliant new venture growing at its original rate for more than three to five years. In fact, if you continue along the same path that made you successful in the first place, you're almost certain to fail. It is easy to change when things are going badly. It is much more difficult—and much more important— to change when things are going well.

What can help you reach the second stage of growth?

A Zigzag Path to the Jackpot

Progress follows a zigzag course. Finding the new vital few parts of reality on which your business relies—to find the new 20 percent of inputs that will yield the precious 80 percent or more of results— requires experimentation and insight.

The 80/20 principle is dynamic. It operates over time. The valuable 20 percent today may not be the vital 20 percent tomorrow. Even if it is, remember *another* even more valuable 20 percent exists within the vital 20 percent you already know about. But to find this gem, you will have to wade through acres of waste. The trivial many always hide the vital few.

An 80/20 Case Study in Retail Evolution

Sam Walton, the founder of Wal-Mart, once said, "Most everything I've done I've copied from someone else." Like most 80/20 individuals, Walton was a voracious copier of successful ideas, but he always applied the ideas to a new arena with his own distinctive traits. And he always continued innovating.

Walton's basic insight was that rural and small-town America was underserved by retailers. The stores were too small and their merchandise too expensive. He set about correcting this.

By the early 1960s, when he was age forty or so, Walton had become the largest independent variety store operator in the United States—and a very rich man. But he was not satisfied.

One day he took two buses, a total of 630 miles each way, to pursue a rumor. He had heard that two Ben Franklin stores, in Pipestone and Worthington, Minnesota, had a self-service system. What he found was one central checkout rather than the then-universal practice of having a cash register at each counter. Self-service was cheaper, and saved the shopper time—but also increased profit because customers paid less attention to the cost of each item. Walton immediately implemented self-service in all his stores.

Despite his success, in 1960 Walton was looking for the second stage of growth. As he later wrote: "After fifteen years we were only doing $1.4 million in fifteen stores. . . . I began looking around hard for whatever new idea would break us over into something with a little better payoff for all our efforts."[1]

At the time, Sears and the A&P had already made a fortune from discount stores. Walton placed a proven idea in a new context; he built large discount stores in new locations, typically small towns where nobody believed the market could sustain a proper discount store.

The first Walton Family Center opened in St. Robert, Missouri, in 1962. Only fifteen hundred people lived there. Yet Walton opened a large store: 13,000 square feet. It was so successful that he quickly enlarged it to 20,000 square feet. Within a year his running rate of sales was $2 million, and he profited more from one store than from all fifteen variety stores two years earlier.

Walton extended the concept when he opened the first real Wal-Mart store in Rogers, Arkansas, in July 1962, with huge placards shouting ALWAYS THE LOW PRICE—ALWAYS. Walton had found his second stage of growth.

Winners Should Breed Prolifically

In business the successful have the greatest opportunity, and obligation, to produce a large number of variants of the success. Most of these variants will fail. A few of them—and it is impossible to predict in advance which few—will succeed.

If you have a successful new venture on your hands, you ought to experiment extensively. That is how you get to the second stage of growth and hit the jackpot.

Yet what do most new enterprises do?

❖ Most new ventures rest on their laurels and never vary the formula that brought them success. The implicit assumption is: Why tinker with the goose that laid the golden eggs? But sooner or later the formula will stop working so well. It hits diminishing returns. At this stage the growth trajectory of the business will be called into question, and its value will plunge.

❖ Sometimes the experiments fail, or are less successful than the original formula. At this stage the founder often gathers his team together and says, "The market has spoken. From now on we stick to our tried-and-tested way of doing things." Experimentation stops. The original route to success works for a time, until it stops working. . . .

Great Business Pioneers Often Screw Up
the Second Stage of Growth

In 1910, 458,000 American families had cars. Ten years later, the number soared to 8,225,000.[2] Henry Ford created this market and by 1920 owned most of it. Yet by 1937, Ford Motor Company had slumped into third place with only 21 percent market share, compared to Chrysler's 25 percent and GM's 42 percent.[3]

Why? Because Henry Ford, the greatest innovator of the 1900s and 1910s, refused to innovate in the 1920s and 1930s. Ford had far fewer new models and far less variety than its rivals.

How can 80/20 individuals keep moving forward when the appeal of their idea seems to be waning?

A cynical person might sell out at the first indication that growth is faltering. However, there is a better option. True 80/20 individuals will attempt countless new variations until they find a new and successful idea. They roll it out until it stops working as well as before, and then start the process all over again. The successful 80/20 individual never stops innovating. Indeed, innovation is the fuel for all lasting 80/20 businesses.

Filofax: Success, Failure, Success, Failure

Filofax was one of the emblematic success stories of the 1980s, driven by David Collischon. But eventually he made the mistake of hiring big-company managers who saddled Filofax with costs it could not carry. In desperation, Collischon turned to me for money and to my partner, Robin Field, for management.

We pursued a classic 80/20 strategy, retrenching Filofax to its few profitable products and customers. We cut prices to fall in line with those of competitors and cut costs to allow us to make money at the new prices. Then we introduced new variants of the most successful products. Within three years, despite eliminating all but a select few Filofax products, volumes had quadrupled and Filofax reached unprecedented profits.

After three years, one of our astute coinvestors sold—for seven times his cost.

Field and I didn't sell then. That was our first mistake. Our second was our failure to innovate. Third, we played the corporate acquisition game.

We had a public success story, and Filofax's stock soared. As consultants we had witnessed this before. We had seen ambitious chief executives buy companies on cheaper ratings and automatically enhance their earnings without producing any basic economic change in the company they acquired. We thought we could do the same.

It started innocently enough. We made six acquisitions, all closely related to the Filofax business: Four were overseas personal organizer firms, and two were UK acquisitions—all six enhanced earnings and were popular with the stock exchange. But when we ran out of closely related companies, we acquired two stationery firms, companies to which we could add little value.

The first stationery company paid for itself within thirty months, but the second, a greeting card company and our biggest move to date, was unpopular with the financial community. It marked down our shares. But, we thought, what do the stock market analysts know? We'd prove them wrong.

The greeting card acquisition was a disaster. Even worse, the takeover led us to neglect innovation in the core Filofax business. We failed to introduce attractive new products that would otherwise have been bought by our loyal customers. Because of this, our growth ended. Our shares, bought initially at between 19 and 45 cents, peaked at $4.20 and then fell below $2.25. In 1998 we sold Filofax for $3.15 per share, roughly the price five years earlier.

Belgo: The Botched Second Stage of Growth

In chapter 6, I described the success of Belgo, the *moules-frites,* modernistic, surreal, "Belgian" restaurant. But I must confess: Belgo's sex life was a failure.

After four years we had two restaurants. The second was a larger, centrally located enterprise, even more successful than the first. Both were big and hugely profitable, but two restaurants does not a chain make.

I knew we had to grow; we had to vary. But somehow I couldn't persuade my working partners to produce enough novel variants. They kept investigating new sites and producing blueprints of new ideas, but none came to fruition. For a booming business, with a return on capital in the 50 to 100 percent range, it was embarrassing to have only two outlets. Was this really a high-growth business with gargantuan potential?

Our variant growth formula consisted of "mini-Belgos," later opened as Bierodromes—smaller restaurants with a very large bar area. Bierodromes proved a great success, but not under our owner-ship.

My partners and I couldn't agree on the growth plan, so we sold the business. It went to the stock market. I made a 17-times return on my money, my partners more. But by botching the second stage of growth, we handed off all that potential for other people to develop and manage.

Looking back, the solution was so simple that I can't believe I missed it. My working partners were best at design and ideas. That was their 20 percent spike. They found the job of locating new sites and getting the restaurants ready an enormous hassle.

What we needed was a new partner, someone skilled at developing new restaurants. We could easily have afforded the best person in the country. We had the cash flow and capital, we had the brand, we had the new formula, we had the reputation, we had the excitement, we had nearly all the ingredients necessary for the second stage of growth. This was the jackpot that got away, and all because we lacked the right 80/20 individual.

Zoffany Hotels: The Second Variant
Is a New Entrepreneurial Structure

My involvement with Zoffany Hotels dates back to 1993. As I write, the formula of buying unfashionable hotels cheaply and increasing their number of bedrooms continues to work very well, but I'm con-cerned about its longevity. For two years, we have been searching for the Zoffany Mark II formula.

Zoffany's uniqueness lies in its entrepreneurial structure. There is no middle management; the partners work directly with the general managers of each hotel in the group, coaching them in the Zoffany business formula.

For some time the two working partners have worried about how far we can push this arrangement, which currently involves ten hotels. We considered operating sixteen hotels with two partners each keep-ing an eye on eight general managers. In the meantime we have been offered a group of forty hotels at an appealing price. But how could we cope with such an expansion? Would we overextend ourselves?

Maybe. But one Zoffany innovation has been to ask two of our top general managers to look after two hotels each. So far, the trial has worked wonders. We are about to give these managers three hotels each and see how that works, and to give another four managers two hotels each.

Of the forty hotels we were offered, we would sell a dozen of them. We would leave another twenty of the remaining twenty-eight alone for the first year, concentrating on the eight hotels that currently account for about 80 percent of the profits of the forty hotels (an 80/20 relationship). We would therefore have eighteen hotels (the old ten and the new eight) to run in the Zoffany way. If each experienced Zoffany general manager took two hotels, we hope it would lead to the second stage of growth. We would be trying a new experiment to build on the existing success, just as a flourishing species spawns new variants in the process of natural selection.

What Will Be Your Second Stage of Growth?

Whether you are a manager or an entrepreneur, don't make the mistake I have often made—imagining that a successful new or remodeled business can keep its formula unchanged for many years. Within three or four years you should be thinking about the next great leap forward, building on the success of your formula while extending and changing it significantly. Experiment until you have found a variant that the market really likes.

Success, not failure, most urgently requires change. Follow the path of natural selection—if it ain't broke, *do fix it!*

Conclusion to Part Two

The 80/20 principle enables people to create more from less: to express their individuality, enrich the world, and lead rewarding lives, ones where they control and cultivate all that is important to them as individuals. It allows them to become 80/20 individuals.

This can always be done. The constraint is not demand, technology, capital, or organization. It is not social, political, or ideological. The only constraint is due to a failure to capitalize on individual human imagination and initiative—of which there is no limit—and repeated experimentation based on varying already successful formulas.

What are we waiting for?

PART THREE

The 80/20 Revolution

CHAPTER 12

From Capitalism
to Individualism

Nothing has been disproved faster than the concept of the "organization man," which was generally accepted forty years ago.
— *Peter Drucker*

T he new way to create wealth is better than the method that dominated the twentieth century. Under the system of managerial capitalism, all serious wealth creation required a large corporation, huge amounts of capital, and masses of managers and workers controlled by the corporation.

The rules have changed. The 80/20 revolution has broken out. Once capital and corporations drove individuals; the tables have turned. Corporations are still important, but the most successful ones now revolve around a few individuals. The corporations exist for the benefit of the individuals. And individuals, not companies or capital, are the crucial ingredient in generating new wealth and growth in the economy.

Although we have a ways to go, we should prepare for a totally new economy, where individuals will be the big winners. The 80/20 revolution, which is leading to the new economy, is as important as the other three transitions in economic history: the agricultural revolution, the Industrial Revolution, and the managerial revolution. These events transformed economies and societies, and over the next two decades so will the 80/20 revolution.

Now for a Genuinely New Economy . . .

We are entering a new economic and social era. New economies arise when a *new and fundamentally better way of generating wealth* is discovered.

New economies don't arise very often. (The alleged "new economy" of 1997–2000, for example, turned out to be a mirage, a mere electronic copy of the "old economy.")

Between 10,000 and 7000 B.C., the *first new economy,* agriculture, gradually replaced the old economy of hunting wild animals and gathering wild fruit and plants. The resulting feudal society prevailed until the Industrial Revolution of the eighteenth century. Then came the *second new economy.* For the first time ever, land generated less wealth than industry. The farm fell to the factory.

The Managerial Revolution

In the late nineteenth century, the *third new economy* emerged as market capitalism faced a new and superior wealth machine. The twentieth century saw a progressive shift from owner-managed, small-scale, national or subnational enterprises to giant national and global corporations run by professional managers and financed through the stock market. If you wanted to get anything serious done in business, you had to be part of an established, large, stock market corporation.

To make sense of the new system, I'll fast-forward again to New York in 1932, as one of the most influential books of the twentieth century just rolled off the presses. In *The Modern Corporation and Private Property,* Adolf Berle and Gardiner Means took American Telephone and Telegraph as their example of the modern, gigantic public corporation:

> With assets of almost four billion dollars, with 454,000 employees, and stockholders to the number of 567,694, this company [American Telephone and Telegraph] may indeed be called an economic empire. . . .

One hundred companies of this size would control the whole of American wealth. . . .

The property owner who invests in a modern corporation . . . surrenders his wealth to those in control of the corporation . . . [to] become merely a recipient of the wages of capital.[1]

Ownership of these mammoth corporations became anonymous and diffused, centered around stock exchanges. Instead of individuals owning and managing corporations, as in the old system, ownership and management were separated, in both cases going into new hands.

The old-style factory owner gave up control to managers when he and his family could no longer fund the voracious demands of their expanding organization. The individual entrepreneur was relegated to the margins of the economy, his functions replaced by industrial managers, fund managers, and stock exchanges. Thus managerial capitalism—an economy dominated by the trinity of large organizations, collective capital providers, and the burgeoning cadre of managers—replaced market capitalism dominated by entrepreneurs and markets.

Why Managerial Capitalism and Large Organizations Flourished

Managerial capitalism triumphed because it held the secret of economic growth: central planning to achieve strategic goals. The large corporation could take a long-term view, by planning to transform an industry and executing its plans through its hierarchy of myriad managers and workers; small entrepreneurs and markets couldn't compete.

For example, under the market system of the 1890s, hundreds of American carmakers, run by owner-managers, turned out small numbers of expensive cars available only to the wealthiest consumers. In 1907, Henry Ford had the vision to "democratize the automobile." To do so he needed to build a huge organization. By the 1920s the Ford Motor Company was churning out millions of cars each year at a fraction of the previous price. Free markets and individual entrepreneurs could never have created such cheap autos or a market large enough for them.

The twentieth-century economy grew mainly because of large organizations and their strategic planning—through massive investment, managerial control, mass production, standardization, and the creation of large markets by lowering costs and prices.

Because this was a better way of creating wealth than had been known before, the economy came to be dominated by large organizations.

There were four key elements in this shift to big organizations:

- ❖ The invisible hand of the market was replaced by the visible hand of management.[2] Large organizations "internalized" or "insourced" market activity: They made rather than bought; they integrated vertically.
- ❖ As a result, central planning and the management hierarchy, rather than random markets, increasingly allocated resources.
- ❖ Ownership was separated from control, now the responsibility of managers. Ownership lost importance.
- ❖ Corporations cornered the means of production, bundling together and monopolizing the wherewithal of enterprise. They controlled technology, brands, access to markets, customers, and capital. In large part, corporations also monopolized business talent.

In an economy dominated by organizations, managers were the great winners. The greatest growth story of the twentieth century was the number and pay of managers. The two other major beneficiaries of managerial capitalism were organized labor and organized savers (pension, insurance, and mutual funds) that increasingly allocated their cash to equities—stock in the giant corporations—and enjoyed the highest returns. At all levels it paid to be organized: to belong to organizations, to place oneself in their slipstream, and to follow a collective approach to making and taking wealth.

The 80/20 Revolution

Since 1980, managerial capitalism has begun to come apart at the seams. The four key elements that marked the transition to managerial capitalism have all spun sharply into reverse:

- ❖ Instead of insourcing from markets, large corporations have started to outsource to markets. They buy rather than make. The best-run and best-positioned corporations specialize in the things they do better than any other corporation, and pass less demanding and lower-return activities into the hands of other corporations.
- ❖ Central planning and management hierarchy are passé. Increasingly markets are allocating resources, as contractual relationships often prove more efficient and flexible than extensive hierarchies. The long reach of the single corporation is being replaced by many smaller, and more focused—and sometimes more profitable or valuable—enterprises.
- ❖ More and more, ownership and control are being reunited. Personal ownership by individuals is becoming important again, as key individuals both run their corporations and own large and valuable stakes in them. The billionaire business magnate has returned with a vengeance.
- ❖ The listed corporation's monopoly on the means of wealth creation is being smashed by the spontaneous actions of myriad entrepreneurs and venture capitalists. You no longer need a large, established corporation to create spectacular wealth. Instead, you can start your own firm, while obtaining technology, brands, market access, customers, and capital from specialist third parties. Although some capital is required, the need for massive physical infrastructure and investment has lessened. You can often use established corporations' excess infrastructure, and you'll also find the amount of investment required is frequently trivial compared to the value that can be created. As I write, Microsoft, the world's third most valuable corporation, is worth $286

billion. Its original external capital need was less than $100,000, well below the level at which stock markets are relevant. In 1986, Microsoft went public, raising a wholly unnecessary $44 million. The return of 6,800 times the 1986 capital (more than three million times the original capital) proves that capital was not the decisive factor in Microsoft's success.

Just as in the three earlier economic revolutions, a superior, novel way of making money has been discovered. The new way follows the 80/20 principle: focus on the few most powerful forces operating in any arena, and especially on the most productive ideas and individuals.

The old way was to aggregate. The new way is to divide, to take averages apart and concentrate on the small parts of the system with extraordinary power to generate wealth.

The old way was to add assets and management structure. The new way is to subtract, compress, flatten, and simplify.

The old way was to piece together an intricate new big picture. The new way is to break up the jigsaw, twisting the few most valuable parts into a new and richer pattern. The 80/20 revolution, by following the 80/20 principle, divides markets and the means of serving them into a much larger number of smaller markets, niches, and activities. The new revolution involves a relentless search for the most profitable customers, products, technologies, employees, partners, and ways of doing business.

The old way was capitalism, a system revolving around capital and large corporations that had massive appetites for capital. The new way revolves around individuals; capital and corporate structures are relatively unimportant. Individualism is replacing capitalism.

If you doubt this, look at the numbers. If capital were less important, its rate of return would fall—which is precisely what has happened. U.S. Federal Reserve Board figures show that the return on capital, now a paltry 4.1 percent, has been falling steadily since the early 1950s. The latest peak was 1996, and even then, the return was much lower than in the 1950s and early 1960s. Also, the share of profits in the economy has fallen from nearly 20 percent in the 1950s to under 8 percent today. Where is the rest of the money? In the hands of individuals.

Just as before, this economic revolution brings a new group of people to the top. The most successful players of the past decade are quite different from those who came before. The gray and reclusive organization men who ruled in the 1950s, 1960s, 1970s, and most of the 1980s, have been replaced by colorful, idiosyncratic, boisterous, daring superstars—people like Jeff Bezos, Richard Branson, Warren Buffett, Larry Ellison, Bill Gates, Andy Grove, Steve Jobs, Anita Roddick, George Soros, and Oprah Winfrey. The new superstars are creators, not inheritors; founders, not followers; entrepreneurs, not managers. They are also very, very rich, and influential to boot. It's no coincidence that capital gains taxes have plummeted at precisely the same time that the billionaire superstars have ascended.

The New Breed of Corporation

Perhaps the most seminal change in the transition to a new economy has already happened: the way most successful corporations now revolve around a few key individuals. Firms such as Amazon, Apple, Berkshire Hathaway, Goldman Sachs, Hewlett-Packard, Microsoft, Oracle, Virgin, and Wal-Mart are personal vehicles for their top executives, usually the founders and a few close associates. These corporations serve the individuals as platforms for their self-expression. The corporations embody the vision and values of their 80/20 leaders.

There is a high correlation between the success of the corporations and the wealth of the top people who have large equity stakes in their firms. For several years the world's richest two people have been Warren Buffett and Bill Gates, thanks to the extraordinary run of success enjoyed by Berkshire Hathaway and Microsoft. In the *Fortune* 500 list for 2001, Gates's 12.3 percent stake in Microsoft was worth $35 billion, while the value of Buffett's 31.2 percent of Berkshire Hathaway— some $32 billion—was almost as mind-boggling. The only compara-

ble personal wealth in America is the $81.6 billion shared by five Wal-
ton family directors of Wal-Mart, another individual-centered corporation (the directors own 40 percent of the company).[3]

There have, of course, always been entrepreneurs such as Andrew
Carnegie, Henry Ford, John and Forrest Mars, John D. Rockefeller,
and Sam Walton, who dominated their corporations and became
hugely rich through their success. But not since the late 1930s has such
a significant chunk of stock market value accrued to personal vehicles
run principally by and for the benefit of the founders and their
coteries.

In 1932, Adolf Berle and Gardiner Means made their names by discovering that two-thirds of America's large corporations were run by
salaried managers rather than entrepreneurs. Had they computed the
market value of these companies, they would have found that a large
majority belonged to what was then the new breed of publicly owned
corporation.

In 2001, traditional corporations still accounted for a substantial
majority of U.S. stock market value. But even at the very top, in the
elite club of the twenty most valuable corporations, there are three
individual-centered companies: Berkshire Hathaway, Microsoft, and
Wal-Mart.

I define an individual-centered corporation as one where at least
one key executive personally owns more than 10 percent of the shares,
or where employees collectively own more than 15 percent. These
three companies satisfy both conditions. A more liberal definition
of the individual-centered corporation—where the directors own
more than 5 percent—would include AOL Time Warner in addition
to the other three. My rule for defining individual-centered corporations is quite stringent. If I included all companies with a billionaire
executive, the list would be much longer.[4]

Do these individual-centered corporations truly represent the
wave of the future? While much more profitable and focused, and less
capital intensive, these three or four individual-centered corporations
may not represent an inevitable trend. But keep in mind that there
were none ten years ago; you had to go down to number 48 in the
1990 *Fortune* 500 list—Apple Computer—to find an individual-

centered corporation. Does this mean that in ten years' time there will be eight or ten such corporations in the *Fortune* 20? Or twenty? Or zero?

The argument cannot be settled statistically. What intrigues me, however, is that the most successful "traditional" organizations— those that have been trading a long time and whose top executives are not founders—have gravitated toward the new breed of corporation. Think of General Electric's remarkable and prolonged resurgence under Jack Welch, who took the company to the top of the *Fortune* ranking. Or of the Coca-Cola Corporation, which enjoyed terrific success under Robert Goizuetta, who became a billionaire in the process. These corporations were not set up as personal vehicles for 80/20 individuals, yet they became, for a time, just that.

What I find extraordinary is how individual-centered corporations have reached into the top drawer of U.S. corporate life. Gaining a foothold at the pinnacle is, of course, much more difficult for individual founders than it is to enjoy success at a lower level. Furthermore, in the rest of the *Fortune* 500, in smaller listed corporations, and in a huge number of private corporations and partnerships, we are witnessing a massive renaissance of individual enterprise led by visionaries who turn existing structures and ideas upside down and create new growth. The 80/20 revolution is transforming business from top to bottom.

What Is Really New about Individual-Centered Corporations?

Is "all" we are seeing a reversion to the typical nineteenth-century business, one owned and run by a family and its clique? That in itself would be a remarkable reversal of economic reality. But history is not repeating itself. A new synthesis is emerging, which combines different aspects of market and managerial capitalism, and which transcends them by creating something new.

Key individuals are dominating the most profitable and successful firms. This is a reversion to an early version of the nineteenth-century norm. Even in the middle of that century, entrepreneurs became increasingly dependent on professional managers and management hierarchies. The prototype professional organization was the railroad, whose period of fastest expansion was 1840–1900. Many entrepreneurs, including Andrew Carnegie and Henry Ford, eventually lost control of their organizations.

There are many reasons that today's founders retain their dominance at the very time when their corporations attain their greatest value. One is that their rise (and possible fall) in value happens faster than ever before. A second reason is that in many cases the need for capital is much more modest. Companies based on so-called intellectual capital depend more on insiders than on external financiers. A third difference between the present and the past is that companies can grow in profits and market value without continually expanding their number of employees and managers. This leads us to another key difference.

Today, 80/20 leaders can change an industry without doing most of the hard work. They can outsource a majority of the activities involved in fulfilling their vision. Of course their corporations still have management hierarchies, but they are controlled by the top individuals. The need for management is chopped up and spread among many suppliers so that the 80/20 leaders are less dependent on their own management machines. When Henry Ford wanted to revolutionize the auto industry, he had to build a corporation to do it all. Today he would simply need the idea, design, and brand of the car; he could subcontract manufacturing, selling, distribution. By all accounts he would have been a great deal happier.

Creative individuals have been liberated from crippling dependence on capital, management, and labor. They no longer need to choose between growing a business and retaining personal control. 80/20 leaders can do both and still have time for family, leisure, sport, art, or philanthropy.

The Broadly Based Economic Rise of the Individual

Today's billionaire industrial bosses are the most extreme examples of 80/20 individuals. Yet the rise of 80/20 individuals is a much longer-standing and broader process, in which creative people from all walks of life are breaking free from collective constraints.

Hollywood is a great example. Hollywood studios in the 1940s were immense, broad enterprises employing writers, producers, directors, stars, cameramen, and other production staff. The corporations made the movies. They distributed them. They owned all the rights. Sometimes they also owned the picture houses (and, essentially, the stars themselves).

In the 1950s and 1960s, however, stars began to flex their muscles. They employed agents and lawyers to negotiate nonexclusive and shorter contracts. Producers, directors, and other individual wealth creators followed suit.

The integrated studio system is now gone. The big studios still exist, but as mere façades. Beneath the proud brands of yesteryear, loose networks of small firms do all the work. Individuals call the shots. The big names own themselves; they keep most of the wealth they generate. In some years Steven Spielberg has earned hundreds of millions of dollars. Top actors—Tom Cruise, Harrison Ford, Tom Hanks—command over $20 million per movie. At humbler levels, other 80/20 individuals, self-employed or working in their own small firms, run the cameras, transport the equipment, provide the makeup; they perform those small but vital tasks acknowledged in the tiny closing credits of a movie.

The sports industry is another example. Most profit from the industry went to TV network corporations, until the value creators in the system staked their claims. The sports leagues were first to demand their share, but before long, individual star players, such as Michael Jordan, began to negotiate for themselves.

Jordan took the process further, capitalizing on his "brand" to market products to fans. Nike originally used Jordan to endorse the Air Jordan brand of athletic shoes; soon he forced Nike to allow him ownership of the brand.

What has happened in Hollywood and sports has also happened throughout every profession. The really juicy returns don't go to corporations or partnerships, but to the few top individuals who add the most value. For example, Joseph Jamial, the world's most highly paid trial lawyer, can make $100 million in a good year.

Below the tip, however, lies the hidden part of the iceberg—a mass of 80/20 individuals who add enormous value, and know it. As business becomes ever more performance-oriented, the 20 percent of individuals who do 80 percent of the really valuable work become more conspicuous. The 80/20 individuals are sometimes able to strike special deals with their employers for greater autonomy or compensation. If this proves impossible—as it often does in large, rule-bound managerial corporations—the 80/20 individuals gravitate to smaller firms of like-minded people, become self-employed, or start their own small company.

Where the billionaires of industry, entertainment, sport, and private practice lead, a much larger number of 80/20 individuals follow. You, too, can grasp control of your destiny by keeping a large share of the wealth and well-being that you create. Simply ensure that your slice of economic life revolves around you.

The Transition from Economic Revolution to New Economy

An economic revolution is the bridge between one economy and its replacement; it is the means of transition to a new economy, not the new economy itself. As Figure 3 shows, a revolution always predates the arrival of the new economy. For example, the Industrial Revolution of 1750–1850 led to market capitalism, but, even in the most advanced economies, market capitalism did not dominate until the second half of the nineteenth century.

At first, the new economy coexists with the old economy, gradually becoming more important. At a certain stage the new economy takes over the majority of the total economy, but this happens only after important changes occur in legal rights and social conventions. At that stage the transition to the new economy accelerates and the new economy becomes dominant, although pockets of the old economy will always persist.

We are clearly experiencing the 80/20 revolution, not the new economy. The old landmarks of managerial capitalism are still intact:

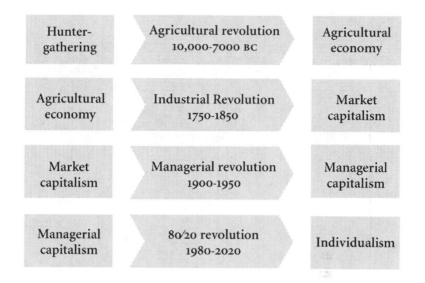

FIGURE 3: Revolutions—The Transition to New Economies

a corporate system that revolves around management hierarchy rather than individuals, and a stock exchange that rewards passive investors as well as those who create new growth. Many 80/20 individuals, such as Rachel and her team, remain content to generate vast swaths of wealth, most of which passes them by. In America and Europe there are hundreds of thousands, perhaps millions, of people like Rachel.

It is probable, however, that within the next two decades, the economy will stop following the old pattern of managerial capitalism. The time will come when most corporations revolve around their key individuals, not the other way round. When this happens, the economy will change abruptly and radically. We will witness a huge wealth transfer to 80/20 individuals and away from institutions, to entrepreneurs and away from "savers" (people who save money and invest in the stock market, a savings account, or another financial institution).

What would a world where individualism replaces capitalism look like—a world where all the Rachels get the rewards they deserve?

CHAPTER 13

What If?

If every person were able to capture the full value of his services,
there would be no corporations.
—*Robert K. Elliott*

What If . . . All 80/20 Individuals Get the Rewards They Deserve?

The 80/20 principle demonstrates that we always underestimate
the power of the few superproductive forces. But we know the
Rachels of this world whip up wonderful wealth. What if they demanded their worth and enforced it, either by moving to start their
own firms or by negotiating a large proportion of the profits they
create?

For example, if half of a typical firm's value comes from creative
individuals rather than the firm itself, half of the annual surplus
should, logically and equitably, go to those 80/20 individuals and not
to shareholders. If half the earnings of corporate America, Europe,
and Japan were suddenly funneled to select employees, those employees would clearly become very rich. But what would happen to stock
markets?

Surely they would collapse. The earnings base would be halved. But
shares would more than halve, because market ratings—price/
earnings ratios—would be affected. The prospects for corporate earnings would suddenly dim, because the trend toward rewarding 80/20
individuals would not be a one-time event; it would become progressively more pronounced. Companies that previously appeared to have

great earnings growth prospects would now have a problematic out-
look. If earnings and price/earnings ratios halved, then stocks would
fall by three-quarters.

Of course this won't happen suddenly. More likely, 80/20 individuals will slowly abandon other people's corporations and start their
own enterprises, a trend that is already evident. But however long it
takes, the end result could be the same.

What If . . . Big Companies Adapt to New Conditions?

Under current conditions, big traditional companies—those where
employees are not substantial owners—are vulnerable. If their 80/20
individuals leave, the growth may stop. Then corporations would still
have their existing profits, but their market rating would fall. Such
firms may become rated like utilities, valued merely for their dividend
yield.

But what if the more progressive big companies adapt to the
changed conditions? Perhaps some of them could mutate into "incubating" firms, willing hosts for new ventures started by 80/20 individuals. In fact many firms already do this as a sideline. But what if the
venturing (incubating) function—already important in many big
firms, including Johnson & Johnson, Intel, and Procter & Gamble—
became their main raison d'être?

Imagine that one of these large corporations acquires experience
and skill in attracting and nurturing 80/20 individuals. It would probably start by setting up its own in-house incubator, encouraging its
own employees to come up with ideas and recruiting 80/20 individuals from outside to join the incubator.

The large corporation would enter a large number of joint ventures with 80/20 individuals, exchanging its expertise and access to
customers for shares in the new entity. The corporation might acquire
a reputation for helping 80/20 individuals set up their own businesses
with a minimum of fuss over legal terms and a maximum interest in
the new venture itself. The market for incubating corporations would
probably evolve its own specialized arenas, with some incubating corporations specializing in particular industries—some in high-tech,

others in services, and others in particular geographies or in helping new ventures globalize.

Some incubating corporations would also provide capital, as GE Capital already does, while others would develop alliances with third-party venture capitalists. Some incubating corporations might even provide management expertise, on a temporary or permanent basis, by assessing and improving the management skills of entrepreneurial teams. Other companies' role might involve facilitating alliances among the many new 80/20 ventures in which they have a stake.

If it is able to constantly attract new 80/20 individuals with prosperous ventures, the incubating corporation may grow its earnings indefinitely. Over time the incubating earnings would dwarf the original business.

In effect, the incubating corporations could become a new type of private equity institution geared toward providing industrial expertise and contacts rather than merely supplying capital.

More companies would exist than ever before. Each incubating corporation may spawn hundreds of new individual-centered enterprises run by 80/20 individuals, each focusing on a particular, narrow sweet spot.

Alongside an increase in the number of firms, we might also see a much greater variety of corporate ownership structures. In addition to conventional publicly listed companies, there might be many private partnerships, small private firms, single-person ventures, and companies set up for specific projects—like the old East India Company—and dissolved once the project is complete.

What If . . . the "Monetization" Music Stops?

Progress is never smooth and simple, or without its downsides. To date, 80/20 individuals have benefited from the credulity of stock markets, allowing firms such as Microsoft to float on high price/earnings multiples, thus "monetizing" the value of the venture for founders and employees (see the appendix for more details).

But what if the arguments in this book became widely accepted? What if people understood that individuals, rather than corporations or capital, add value, and that any valuable corporation, even one such as Microsoft, can be vulnerable to the defections of key 80/20 individuals?

What if the defections of people like Jeff Hawkins and Donna Dubinsky—the inventors of the PalmPilot, who fell out with the corporation that acquired them and set up Handspring, their own new venture—became commonplace rather than exceptional?

What if Microsoft investors realized more fully how dependent on Bill Gates and his coterie they have become, and dumped the stock?

What if the best employees, especially newer or younger ones, demanded new and more valuable stock options as the current ones plunge?

What if the institutional shareholders of Microsoft resisted a further transfer of wealth from them to employees?

What if the defection of the brightest young people at Microsoft caused it to lose market share?

It is not difficult to paint a picture of a downward spiral, where a yawning gap opens up between Microsoft's 80/20 individuals and its passive shareholders. In good times everyone overlooks possible causes of conflict. In bad times everyone becomes vociferous in advancing and defending their own corner.

It is not impossible to imagine Bill Gates reluctantly siding with his own people against Microsoft's institutional shareholders. In my negative scenario, he might conclude that it is impossible to salvage Microsoft's falling share price, and that his reputation and professional career would benefit from moving a team of its best 80/20 individuals to a new corporation.

If that happened, the magic monetization music—the ability of firms dependent on a few highly talented and mobile individuals to maintain the high stock rating as if they were like the previous species of high-growth firms, where the company itself was the real source of value—would surely shudder to an abrupt halt.

Once bitten, forever shy. Never again would investors believe it sensible to give an individual-centered firm a rating of 20 to 100 times its annual earnings when the source of those earnings might cut bait within a few years or even months.

Of course, the likelihood that Microsoft will sink is very slim. But it's more plausible that, over the next twenty years, a high-flying new company's 80/20 individuals will stage a mutiny against passive investors. It's likely that a firm that investors once believed was worth 20 to 100 times current earnings would tank once its 80/20 individuals jumped ship. One such high-profile "disaster" could be all it takes for investors to scramble for the lifeboats.

What If . . . Cash Becomes King and the Stock Market Becomes Unimportant?

If 80/20 employees obtain a large minority, or a majority, of corporate profits, or if the monetization music stops, then stock markets may not only slump—they could become irrelevant.

If companies' price/earnings ratios fell far enough, they'd become attractive candidates for going private, removing themselves from the stock exchange. Already private buyouts are at their highest level, barring only the LBO (leveraged buyout) explosion of the late 1980s. In 2000, for example, Seagate Technologies, the world's biggest maker of disk drives, went private in a $20 billion deal.[1]

Many listed companies have poor growth prospects, low market ratings, but a very high cash flow. The stock market is not the best place for such companies to be. As Larry Shulman of the Boston Consulting Group says, "A public corporation is a relatively risky and inefficient vehicle for accumulating cash."

A more economic alternative in a low-interest-rate climate is to pay off the public shareholders, reduce the equity base to a fraction of its current size, and fund the gap by taking on debt. The cash flow can later be used to extinguish the debt. Meanwhile, the interest paid to the banks nicely reduces taxes. Even without a buyer for the company, repeated "recapitalizations"—paying off the old debt and then loading the company with new debt—mean that cash can be taken out of the company.

Yet in this scenario, in addition to low-growth companies, high-growth companies, which comprise a greater chunk of the total value of the stock market, will also go private. High-growth companies run by 80/20 individuals could become unattractive to the public market because of their dependence on these individuals. 80/20 individuals would eat into earnings previously reserved for shareholders, but another danger exists: that the engine of profitability—the 80/20 individuals—could disappear without warning.

Faced with this dual pincer attack, passive shareholders might lose their nerve, sell the shares, slash the firm's market rating, and make it attractive for 80/20 individuals to buy back full ownership of the corporation, using debt to buy in the shares that employees don't already own.

If this happened on a big enough scale, the stock market would not merely sink like a stone; it would empty! Existing stocks would disappear while new public offerings would dry up. Investors would want old-style corporations they could depend on—those that promised growth without a dependence on a few individuals. These corporations would become increasingly rare, restricted to low-growth and low-profit "utilities" in the low-return areas 80/20 individuals avoid.

Perhaps public markets would stick to stocks offering exposure to 80/20 enterprises but in a controlled and relatively low-risk way. Examples of such stocks might be old-style firms such as GE or Johnson & Johnson that became incubating corporations with a heavy dash of venture capital. Private equity itself would increase in importance, possibly becoming larger than public equity, although private equity firms might even evolve into attractive investment vehicles on the stock market.

One side effect of any stock market decline would be a drop in the number of acquisitions of firms by other firms, as they are often funded by "paper"—new shares in the acquirer—which would have much less value than before. High valuations for acquired firms would also seem suspicious as earnings, and implicit price/earnings ratios, came under greater scrutiny. Why bother to acquire an asset whose value is likely to fall over time?

Venture Capital and Private Equity Evolve to
Back 80/20 Individuals

As private equity and venture capital continue to expand, their character might also shift. New venture capital institutions could specialize in helping 80/20 individuals form joint ventures with their former employers. Some new private equity firms might tackle the opportunity from the other end, by helping large traditional firms become incubating corporations, supplying semicaptive capital to the new 80/20 enterprises. Other new venture capital houses may emerge as brokers, foraging for joint ventures between traditional firms and 80/20 individuals, and helping to put such deals to bed.

There might be a flowering of gentler venture houses, tailoring deals to the needs of the new teams of individuals. These houses would tout the "happiest" deals, offering 80/20 individuals lower leverage, risk, stress, and financial commitment, while still providing attractive (though not earth-shattering) returns. Compared to traditional private equity deals, the 80/20 individuals would have lower upside; they might make a few millions less but would be happier as every other need was met.

We may see an expansion of organized and semiorganized "angel" finance. Rich individuals may band together in loose networks to back 80/20 individuals. Some venture capital houses may focus on providing ready-made deals for angels, taking on the burden of due diligence and financial structuring. Many 80/20 individuals who have already made one fortune may go on to become sponsors of a whole string of new 80/20 enterprises.

Cash Becomes King

With increasing wariness about putting high price/earnings multiples on corporations, and decreasing stock market dominance, we may see a change in the economy's ultimate measure of value.

This has happened before. Under feudalism, what mattered was the number of serfs or slaves one owned, and the value and income from land. With the advent of early market capitalism, the balance sheet—the assets owned by the corporation—became the most important financial yardstick.

In the twentieth century, the profit-and-loss statement became more important than the balance sheet. Earnings were king. Then in the second half of that century, something else happened: Earnings mattered less than the market capitalization of the company, the total market value (earnings multiplied by an arbitrary number, and the price/earnings ratio).

Although there were fluctuations, as the twentieth century wore on, two clear trends emerged: Price/earnings ratios tended to rise, and also to become more volatile. The gap between earnings and market value became more pronounced, but also less reliable. Increasingly, value came to reside, or at least appeared to reside, not in today's cash, not even in today's earnings (which, again, became more detached from cash flows), but in the stream of earnings that might materialize in the future.

These trends always seemed to be modeled after the emperor's new clothes. People believed in ever-escalating valuations because everybody else did. The valuations were built on shifting sands. Not only were there fewer cents of earnings and assets to support each dollar of apparent value, but everyone also turned a blind eye to the evidence piling up that the source of the earnings was mobile individuals—not the corporation and its assets.

The detachment of valuations from real cash and the real source of value is bound to end at some stage. What might the trigger for the change be?

It could be intellectual, but it could also be demographic. The stock market booms of the 1980s and 1990s coincided with the hump of baby boomers, then in their forties and fifties, shoveling money into shares in anticipation of their retirement. Equities as a proportion of household financial assets in the United States rose from 15 percent in 1985 to 34 percent in 1999. Their demand for shares raised their price and average price/earnings ratios. Whenever the stock market dipped and price/earnings ratios became more sensible, renewed demand from private investors, brainwashed into "buying on dips," moved the markets back up into the stratosphere.[2]

The proportion of people in their forties and fifties will continue to rise in the United States until 2006, when it will peak at just over 40 percent of the population. It will then decline quite sharply until 2024. During this period of 2006 to 2024, if the retired baby boomers sell shares, particularly if they start to slip for reasons related to 80/20 enterprise, any fall in share prices could become an avalanche. The net buyers from 1985 to 2006 could be expected to become net sellers in the future, but if markets fall for nondemographic reasons, baby boomers would rush for the exit, falling over each other to sell before their retirement dreams fade.

The effect could be a restoration of a sensible basis of valuation: Cash would replace earnings (which are merely a promise of cash in the future), and market capitalizations (a pyramid of hopeful expectations about earnings long into the future). Anything that calls into question the substance of those hopes may prompt an abrupt flight into cash.

Cash is the only measure understood and trusted by venture capitalists and private equity financiers. They measure their success by two benchmarks, the internal rate of return (the average compound annual return on cash) and the cash-to-cash ratio (the number of times by which any investment multiplies the cash invested). Cash is not a measure suited to the stock market. The rise of cash and private equity, and the decline of the stock market, would be a piece of the 80/20 revolution.

Equity Becomes Unimportant

Even private equity could become anachronistic. Private equity houses, venture capital, and angel finance may experience a gradual shift from owning equity—a share of permanent ownership in enterprises—to owning temporary debt instruments. Instead of owning a share of the business and hoping to increase their investment when it is sold, venture capitalists might set a fixed annual return that could be paid back by 80/20 individuals at any time.

Here is an example of how it might work. Imagine I set up a new 80/20 enterprise that needs $1 million of capital. Traditionally, I would give perhaps 75 percent of the ownership to a venture capitalist providing the $1 million. In the new world, the venture capitalist gets no shares, but receives "interest" of 50 percent a year on the $1 million, compounded annually. The interest in the first year would be $500,000 and, if I could not pay this back, it would then be added to the principal, so that the second year's interest would be $750,000 (50 percent on $1.5 million). However, as my venture generated cash, I would repay the venture capitalist while keeping 100 percent of the company. The venture capitalist would probably own the company until he was paid back, but would have to give up his shares once repaid.

Why would this change suit the new world? If the chance to float a company on the stock exchange dried up, and if acquisitions became difficult or unfashionable, it might be problematic to secure the "exit" that private equity houses want. They would have to get their return another way: from the cash flow of the business itself.

80/20 individuals would be more attached to their businesses than traditional entrepreneurs; partly from choice, but partly also from necessity. If the option of getting rich quick by selling out after a few years faded, 80/20 individuals would pay increasing attention to making their business a place for their long-term careers. Without outside shareholders, it would become legitimate and socially approved to follow nonfinancial as well as financial criteria. Many business founders already have nonfinancial objectives—they want their business to endure and make progressively greater contributions to the world—but feel obliged to soft-pedal these objectives or keep them in the closet for fear of offending financial backers. The inherent conflict between owners and executives would disappear if executives had 100 percent ownership. 80/20 individuals would be free to choose between financial and nonfinancial goals, and between short- and long-term imperatives.

If venture capitalists increasingly targeted a known and smooth annual return on their money, and if the success rate were assessed statistically, then retail funds from ordinary private investors may be attracted to this type of investment. The venture capitalist might target a 40 percent annual return and, after losses, receive 20 percent on a fairly reliable basis. The ordinary retail investor might then receive 10 percent a year, with the balance going to the individual venture capitalists. A new form of "quasi-venture capital" might gradually replace stock exchange investment, or even saving via bank deposits.

The Decline of Capital?

In a world of 80/20 enterprise, capital would no longer be a commodity. Its importance would decline as large and very profitable individual-centered businesses were built, like Microsoft, with little or no capital.

As capitalism fades, the rate of return on capital will continue to fall. True, there will be an explosion of new 80/20 ventures, most requiring some capital and rewarding their backers handsomely. On the other hand, a surfeit of emigré capital from the public markets will be looking for a new home, a glut of capital chasing too few deep uses. Probably, capital will earn high returns only if it is unusually lucky or if it offers an additional ingredient—such as practical help for 80/20 enterprises.

This would mark a major change from twentieth-century experience, when passive capital invested in the stock market saw extraordinary returns. The most popular and reliable way to get rich in that world was to save and invest in the market. As the century closed, broad middle-class prosperity in the developed countries rested less on work than on investment in the stock market, which required little or no skill from the savers.

Any large-scale downgrading of stock markets' size and value would have profound economic and social consequences, especially if linked to a transfer of wealth from passive investors to 80/20 individuals.

While sustainable wealth in the real economy would increase, the perceived wealth of most people—and indeed their real wealth, as measured by instruments such as shares—might fall rather sharply.

Effects on the Economy

The effect on the economy as a whole due to a market fall that occurs gradually over several decades might be muted, but individual fortunes could be transformed. On the other hand, if stock markets crash and fail to recover, we could enter a serious depression unless monetary authorities prepare for the crash by pumping liquidity into the economy.

A world where 80/20 enterprise is prevalent should raise employment levels, real (nonfinancial) market activity, and international trade, and, ultimately, put a damper on economic swings caused by financial speculation. We could also see a more level playing field for emerging economies as capital becomes more available (because of its glut in the developed world) and as multinational corporations lose their ability to snap up and control successful local enterprises.

What If . . . Partnerships Become Popular?

If 80/20 enterprises constitute a majority of the economy's profits, ambitious young people may start work as employees in order to gain experience, contacts, and access to powerful ideas. But they will aim to be 80/20 individuals, with serious ownership, by age thirty. The corporate career will become a memory.

More new ventures will spring up than ever before. Nearly all will be 80/20 enterprises. Before long, a majority of firms will be 80/20 ventures.

If listing on the stock exchange or selling to another corporation ceases to be the typical route for successful ventures, then most 80/20 firms may choose to become partnerships. It would be unrealistic to expect this as long as it is possible to monetize earnings through flotation or sale.

However, if these routes become unavailable there would be few advantages—and many disadvantages—to having outside investors. It would be wiser to build a partnership, which encourages collegiate behavior for the long run, attracting people who want to build a lengthy career. Partnerships eliminate conflict between owners and executives, and create an environment where one generation of partners benefits from the previous generation and builds for the next.

Instead of having a one-off windfall when selling or floating, 80/20 partners would gradually become rich by sharing in annual profits. With decreased capital needs, most profits could be consumed annually rather than retained.

The typical longevity of small enterprises would also increase, further exaggerating the idiosyncrasies of particular ventures. There would be more emphasis on the quality of working life and autonomy for individuals. Partners would set working conditions that suit themselves and would attract other 80/20 individuals by giving them freedom in all aspects of their work. Differences in the manner, place, and time that people work would increase. Self-employed people have long been able to choose their working hours and integrate their home and work lives as they please. Whether they are partners in their own organization or continue to work as employees, 80/20 individuals will claim these liberties. The current trend of longer working hours will probably also be reversed, as individuals use the 80/20 principle to produce more and better work in less time.

Whether they form partnerships or not, employees may generally prefer to work for 80/20 enterprises. The ethos will tend to be more personal, with less corporate bureaucracy. An 80/20 venture's high profits and lack of obligations to outside shareholders will also lead to higher pay.

What If . . . Big Becomes Passé?

We might reasonably expect the spirit of 80/20 enterprise to overflow into the rest of society.

In the twentieth century, nonbusiness organizations mimicked the megacorporations. Gigantic public bureaucracies arose at city, national, and international levels. Volunteer organizations followed suit, seeking to extend their size and reach. There were few objective advantages from size and many drawbacks. Still, the unspoken assumption remained: If this was the model for successful business, it must be the model for the rest of society.

But if the typical successful business enterprise became a medium-size partnership, owned entirely by its executives and reflecting the individual character of its founders, what lessons would the rest of society draw?

Imagine that nonbusiness organizations re-formed around exceptional individuals, 80/20 individuals whose particular bent was creating well-being rather than wealth! By following the 80/20 principle, government and the social sector would radically decentralize, fragmenting into more focused units. Some of the new 80/20 social enterprises might specialize locally or by activity while others might be based entirely around individuals or cells of creative people.

Possibly we would see the large-scale emergence of individual social entrepreneurs, 80/20 individuals whose mission is to increase well-being by using powerful ideas and working them out through a variety of joint ventures with focused nonprofit entities. These 80/20 individuals would attract public money and private donations to achieve specific results, but contract out the work to existing organizations.

Individuals today generally work through organizations, not as single catalysts. In the future, individuals and small groups of individuals will be influential without needing to build an organization.

For example, if I wanted to end homelessness and vagrancy in San Francisco, I would announce my objective and the way I believed it could be achieved (for example, by tailoring rehabilitation programs to the needs of homeless drug addicts). I would canvass for partners—both individuals and other organizations—and for funds. If I were successful, I would encourage friends in other cities to adopt and adapt the distinctive approaches that had worked in San Francisco. Successful 80/20 individuals would progressively attract funds but avoid building up their own organizations.

Existing welfare and nonprofit agencies would be "chopped up" into several smaller units and, as in business, become interconnected with many other entities through strategic alliances. Schools, for instance, might become more specialized, but swap teachers, students, and databases to help improve one another's performance. Students would have much greater freedom to focus on the subjects that really excited them and would have much greater control over their life at school. Individuals—students and staff—would achieve more because they would concentrate on what they do best.

What If . . . Individuals Took Charge of Their Destiny?

In a landscape dominated by large organizations, few people stamp their mark on the world. Most people are content to leave their fate to others—to existing organizations—whose pattern is already determined. They lend their lives to the past.

The 80/20 revolution will end the era of personal passivity. In a world run by 80/20 individuals, business and society will revolve around individuals. Everyone will be challenged to take charge of his or her own destiny. Ordinary people who want to achieve extraordinary results will use the 80/20 principle to do so. Affirming and celebrating the individuality of every human being and his or her role in enriching the world will become the norm, not the exception.

All previous revolutions, including the communist ones, had little room for ordinary people. Revolutions focused on "masses," not individuals. The 80/20 revolution is different because it elevates individuals above organizations. For most of the twentieth century, ordinary people were cannon fodder, factory fodder, or, if fortunate, office fodder. In the twenty-first century, for the first time ever, individuals are more important than classes or organizations. The freedom to become a productive individual by choosing to contribute to society on one's own terms is now universal.

The 80/20 principle can help everyone get more of what he or she wants with less effort, by working with the grain of the universe and not against it. By using powerful ideas, and the practices that work best for each one of us, we make the most of our lives.

A better future—a better society, and a better life for every individual—can be created by the conscious efforts of millions of productive 80/20 individuals.

The future depends on improving the quality and integrity of our dreams, on using the 80/20 principle to plug into the universe's creativity grid, and on fulfilling our own unique potential.

The future will be made by 80/20 individuals. Shouldn't you be one of them?

The Roots and Ramifications of the Revolution

> Now this is not the end. It is not even the beginning of the end.
> But it is, perhaps, the end of the beginning.
>
> —*Winston Churchill*

This appendix will appeal to readers who like to relate theory and practice, and who are amenable to heresy. First, I'll explain the theoretical and practical roots of the 80/20 revolution in greater detail than in the main text. Next, I'll share the radical and somewhat uncomfortable possible effects of the revolution—particularly the threat to the stock exchange system that so many of us have used to supplement our income and increase our wealth.

Sadly, as I have predicted since the beginning of 2000, the heights of the stock market at the turn of the millennium are unlikely to be reached again. The replacement of capitalism by individualism implies a long-term, continual decline in prices on the stock exchange. The decline in share prices, according to the theory of the 80/20 revolution, is not driven by temporary difficulties, such as recession, managerial fraud, terrorism, or war.

The real cause of the decline is a long-term change in the nature of wealth creation.

The 80/20 revolution implies that wealth is now created more by individuals than by corporations and capital, and that 80/20 individuals will gain a progressively greater share of national income, as corporations lose correspondingly. If corporations' earnings continually decline through leakage of income to individuals, it is difficult to see how the stock market can do anything other than decline, and on a much greater scale than ever before.

The Rise and Fall of Managerial Capitalism

The 80/20 revolution—the process by which individualism replaces capitalism—can best be understood by comparing and contrasting the rise of managerial capitalism (the economy that is still dominant, but losing ground) and the rise of individualism. Two tables summarize the changes.

TABLE 1: *Milestones in the Rise of Managerial Capitalism*

1840s–1860s Major construction of railroads. Railroads require management coordination and collective ownership. Invention of the managed, hierarchical, large public corporation.

1860–1900 Major technological innovation, including wireless telegraph, the telephone, gas, electricity, and refrigeration. Technology, management, and mass production lead to large organizations. Large public-sector organizations proliferate in America and Europe: the post office, armies, navies. In Europe, gas and electricity companies are typically owned by states or municipalities.

1870–1901 Andrew Carnegie reorganizes the steel industry based on maximum scale and continuous operation of steel mills. In 1901, U.S. Steel acquires Carnegie Steel to create a massive corporation.

1905–25 Henry Ford turns the automobile industry from a fragmented market with hundreds of producers into a mass-market duopoly.

1917 Lenin seizes power in Russia and creates an organizational state, modeled on Fordist lines of industrialization, mass production, large organizations, and central management.

1900–45 Organizations acquire national scope and replace or limit markets by "insourcing" activities that used to be provided by outside firms.

Corporations increase the numbers of employees and capital employed. Market activity is reduced through industrial consolidation. International trade falls.

1932 Publication of *The Modern Corporation and Private Property* by Adolf Berle and Gardiner Means. They celebrate "the new modern quasi-public corporation": "American industrial property, through the corporate device . . . [is] being thrown into a collectivist hopper wherein the individual owner is steadily being lost in the creation of a series of huge industrial oligopolies." They announce that two-thirds of American industry is controlled collectively and identify the trend toward "the separation of ownership from control."

1933–34 Hitler takes over Germany and institutes complete state direction of industry through gigantic public and private corporations.

1941 James Burnham invents the term "manager" in his influential book *The Managerial Revolution*. "The transition from capitalist society to managerial society is already well under way."

1945–80 American (and European) multinational corporations gain unprecedented reach and economic power. The free enterprise organization proves greatly superior to the public-sector version. International trade soars.

1960–2000 The invention of the hostile takeover enables well-regarded corporations to become larger and more complex.

1970–90 The growth of diversified corporations operating in many industries.

1970–90 A few large Japanese multinational corporations achieve notable success, using highly developed central planning within each corporation.

TABLE 2: *Milestones in the Decline of Managerial Capitalism and the Rise of Individualism*

1937–48 A series of important books celebrate individualism and warn of the dangers of collectivism to the human spirit. Particularly influential are *Anthem* (1938, 1946) and *The Fountainhead* (1943) by Ayn Rand, *The Road to Serfdom* (1944) by F. A. Hayek, and *Animal Farm* (1946), and *1984* (1949) by George Orwell.

1950–65 Hollywood stars break the studio system and capture value as individuals.

1959 Peter Drucker coins the term "knowledge workers." New knowledge-based jobs, he says, require a different mind-set. Knowledge workers are self-managing and mobile.

1970–2000 Business school graduates and other ambitious individuals turn from large corporate careers to lucrative professions (accounting, consulting, investment banking, and venture capital) or to starting their own enterprises.

The rise of venture capital and private equity provide individuals with backing for new ventures.

1975 Microsoft is founded by Bill Gates and Paul Allen. It requires minimal capital.

1975–2000 The growth of leveraged buyouts (LBOs) and buyins (LBIs) enables individuals to mutate from managers to principals. Sports and pop stars become individual enterprises. Bowie bonds issued, giving entitlement to a share of megastar David Bowie's future earnings.

1980–2000 The star system and "winner takes all" become important in the general professions. Large business starts to lose market share to small and medium-sized enterprise.

Companies focus on "core businesses" and sell or close the rest. Diversification becomes a dirty word—"diworsification."

1980–90 Microsoft becomes an important corporation and the prototype for a new owner-managed enterprise: highly focused, highly profitable, highly valuable, with relatively few employees, assets, or capital employed.

1986 Microsoft goes public, not to raise money but to monetize the value of employee ownership.

1990 C. K. Prahalad and Gary Hamel publish a landmark article, "The Core Competence of the Corporation," in the May–June *Harvard Business Review*. They advocate a focus on learning rather than physical assets and tell corporations to exit activities that don't use core competencies.

1990–2000 "Downsizing" and "empowerment" become all the rage. For the first time, most large organizations start progressively reducing their headcount and number of management layers. The separation of ownership from control is progressively reversed, as owner-managed enterprises become an increasing proportion of U.S. stock market value. This trend survives the "Internet bubble" of 1998–2000.

"Outsourcing" becomes a major trend, reversing a century of insourcing and decreasing the reach and importance of management hierarchies. Strategic outsourcing—where key activities are undertaken by outside firms—becomes popular. Strategic alliances take off. The typical large corporation had zero alliances in 1989; ten years later it had thirty. Accenture estimates that alliances will represent $25 trillion of revenues by 2004. Academics find that by using strategic outsourcing and strategic alliances, the old trade-off between markets and corporations can be transcended. We can have both corporate planning and market efficiency by breaking down the boundaries between organizations. Management hierarchies lose importance and orchestration across companies, without management authority becomes crucial.

1992 Peter Drucker announces "the *Fortune* 500 is over." Tom Peters publishes *Liberation Movement*, praising disorganization.

1993–2000 Under pressure from investors, large firms increasingly break themselves up into two or more firms. The value of "breakups" grows rapidly and in 1996 exceeds $100 billion.

1996 Al Ries publishes *Focus*, showing that focused corporations are

more profitable than less-focused ones, and that a decade of
U.S. "unfocusing" is being corrected.

Microsoft reaches a market value of $86 billion. It has less
than $1 billion in net fixed assets.

1996–2000 "Virtual corporations" multiply. Whole industries become
more virtual as strategic outsourcing becomes typical.

1997 Three different books with the same title, *Intellectual Capital,*
are published. A consensus emerges that brainpower is more
important than physical assets and financial capital.

2000 The Boston Consulting Group asserts that in talent-based industries "the key unit of value creation is the *individual*" (their
emphasis), not the corporation or the team.

2001 Microsoft reaches a market value of $286 billion.

A New Synthesis of Academic Theory

Over the past decade or so, management gurus and academics have
gushed out a flood of fads and fancies with bewildering speed and variety. We've seen core competencies, focus, downsizing, delayering,
empowerment, business process reengineering, outsourcing, supply
chain management, "co-opetition," strategic alliances, parenting theory, and virtual corporations. As the gurus move to carve out their
own proprietary intellectual niches, they tend to stress the novel and
exclusive elements of their ideas.

Yet what if these competing theories are all part of one larger business trend, so that, like the blind Indian men describing an elephant,
each writer has grasped one piece of the puzzle? What if the common
element behind all their insights is the decline of managerial capitalism and the rise of individualism? What if the common factor is the
application of the 80/20 principle: the search for the most productive
uses of ideas, people, and capital?

One useful recent academic theory explains how to transcend the
traditional trade-off between market efficiency and corporate effectiveness. We can have both.

By breaking down barriers between competing corporations
and markets, 80/20 corporations can pursue strategic, long-term

goals, while using markets and other organizations to fulfill them.

For example, Dell Corporation has a purpose: to provide business users with a huge range of different PCs—through direct selling, at lower cost than through traditional retail stores. A market could not organize itself to fulfill such a purpose.

In the old days a firm such as Dell would have owned and managed a large number of assembly and subassembly operations to meet customers' needs. But Dell never has. Instead, it uses a number of subcontractors who perform all of the manufacturing operations. Dell uses another set of subcontractors to deliver its products to customers. All it does is take orders from customers via the phone, fax, and Internet. Then it orchestrates the process of providing custom-made computers.

Why use the word "orchestrate"? Why not "manage"? To differentiate between "internal management," where managers use a hierarchy to get things done, and "external orchestration," where executives organize the process using market relationships rather than a management hierarchy.

There is a hierarchy within Dell, but it is a short one and relates only to a minority of the activity that Dell controls—the hierarchy relates to the people who take orders for computers, who are Dell's employees. For every Dell employee, several other people do work for Dell but are employed by other firms. Dell controls a system that pursues its strategic objectives, yet more of the activity happens outside Dell than inside.

The relationship between Dell and its subcontractors is a market relationship, yet also a strategic relationship. It is not a one-time deal; if the subcontractor performs well, the relationship may become permanent.

This system offers Dell and its customers most of the advantages of markets—efficiency, responsiveness, and the ability to weed out underperformers—with the advantages of corporations—strategic planning, organizing, and effectiveness in pleasing customers.

Most of the superprofitable new corporations that have emerged since 1975, from Nike to Microsoft, have had this in common: They focus on a few activities but organize a system that stretches far beyond their corporate boundaries. They have few employees compared to their revenues and profits.

What Happens Inside Corporations Has Become Less Important

Without most people realizing it, much has happened to the corporation and its role. Once, elements within the corporation mattered: its technology, know-how, factories, warehouses, sales channels, capital, and the actions of employees, coordinated by the management hierarchy. The company was rich and powerful because it did things.

Now the emphasis is quite different. What matters now is what happens "between" or "outside" corporations.

Corporations used to be powerful because they bundled together a large number of different activities and attributes. They had proprietary technology, and access to markets and customers. Within their walls they had all kinds of experts and experienced managers. They had ideas. They had a corporate way of doing things, their own distinctive culture. They had access to special information and secrets kept from the outside world, often hidden from the owners of the corporations themselves (for example, particularly profitable businesses or income streams that managers kept a lid on). They had plenty of capital and access to any further capital that might be required. They had jealously protected brands. They owned a large number of things, including other firms.

This bundle of attributes had elements of both a monopoly and a puzzle. A monopoly because if you wanted to get anything serious done in business, you needed a large corporation. A puzzle because although the corporation was clearly valuable, since it generated increasing streams of profits, it was never clear what the source of the profits was. Was it the brand, the technology, the assets, the customer base, the culture, the knowledge workers, or the managers that really generated the value? Nobody bothered to ask the question, because as long as the corporation's attributes fed off and reinforced one another, there was no point in trying to prioritize them. The puzzle was related to the monopoly; if you couldn't separate the elements of value in practice, why try to do so in theory?

The New à la Carte Menu of Wealth Creation

Corporations are losing their monopoly on the elements of value. Value is escaping from the corporate nexus and becoming increasingly à la carte.

Technology and ideas are more transparent, for example, via the World Wide Web. It is easier—and usually cheaper—to access other corporations' customer bases, for example through concessions in department stores, or renting a list of customers. Ideas are becoming liberated from corporations—being carried out by individuals who leave to start a new business, and cross-pollinated by the ever-burgeoning armies of consultants and information providers. Accounting standards are being tightened, forcing corporations to reveal the true sources of their profits. Capital is available from third parties; from venture capitalists, for instance. Even high quality brands like Virgin are available to outsiders, provided the terms are right.

Nobody deliberately set out to take away the corporation's monopoly on the elements of value, or to make them separately available. In fact it could never have happened if corporations hadn't allowed it. And still, few people have even noticed that it has happened.

Why did it occur? For greater efficiency. The economy is evolving toward more productive, transparent, and variegated ways of conducting enterprise, where the elements of value in the economy can be identified, separated, and freely traded. This is a benign process, occurring piecemeal and without any overall plan, because it raises economic returns and growth. The process involves the progressive application of the 80/20 principle: "de-averaging" returns and looking everywhere for the highly productive forces, allowing value to flow freely to and from these forces.

Corporate Boundaries and Hierarchies Become Less Important, Individuals More Important

I'll revisit the academic theory about markets and organizations. Professors are saying that the management hierarchy is less important in creating value than it used to be.

The new growth systems are created by ideas and people, with less need for corporations, extensive management hierarchy, and heavy capital requirements.

This is tremendous news for individuals. In the old model, what mattered was the corporate hierarchy, tied to a bundle of corporate assets and attributes—the individual was dispensable. In the 80/20 model what matters is the idea for a better economic system and the ability to orchestrate—to influence and control people outside your organization. Here the individual is essential.

This theory fits the facts. As Wharton professor Peter Cappelli says, "It used to be that you could always walk out the door, but you couldn't do outside what you could inside of a company. I could leave with an idea but I could never make it happen. Now, that's not the case."[1]

Value Is Created Using the 80/20 Principle

The way to generate wealth is to isolate the few most powerful and profitable forces and leverage them fully, not just at one time but continually.

Over time, each economic system (each idea, technology, product, service, individual, team, corporation, supply chain, or economy) that expands does so through superior value creation, by providing more valuable output with less valuable input.

Serious value growth results from a never-ending stream of experiments, a combination of new ideas, the selection of the best variations of an enterprise, and the relocation of resources from the least productive parts of a system to the most productive parts.

However creative a system is, a minority of components will always be several times more fecund than others; constant improvement, therefore, is always possible.

The 80/20 principle unites and describes all the practical and evident components of change that once seemed unrelated and whose significance was underestimated.

When corporations focus on fewer products, services, and activities, they are following the 80/20 principle. They "de-average" by focusing on the vital few products and activities.

When corporations outsource, they follow the 80/20 principle. They de-average.

When corporations create a new business system that involves several other corporations and leads to higher returns on capital, they follow the 80/20 principle. They de-average.

When corporations break themselves into two or more new, separate corporations, they follow the 80/20 principle. They de-average.

When corporations confine themselves to activities using their core competencies, they follow the 80/20 principle. They de-average.

When a manager and her small team remodel a business, focusing on the really profitable activities and dramatically increasing the return on capital as a result, they follow the 80/20 principle. They de-average.

When managers stay within a company, but gain autonomy and a share of the new profits they create, they follow the 80/20 principle. Instead of wealth going straight to shareholders or managers, a greater share of wealth goes to those who create it. The distribution of wealth is de-averaged.

When managers start a joint venture within or outside their own company, they share in the new wealth they create. Instead of a simple share in annual profits, the 80/20 individuals (the managers) also gain a share in ownership so they will benefit if their unit is sold in the future. Once again, returns are de-averaged in accordance with the 80/20 principle.

When new ventures try to identify the most profitable parts of a market and build a new business around it, they follow the 80/20 principle. They de-average, causing a smaller, more profitable business definition to emerge. The result is a great number of smaller firms, an increase in total wealth, and a transfer of wealth from old to new firms.

When the best individuals from a firm decide to set up a business together, they follow the 80/20 principle. They are likely to demonstrate that fewer employees can generate more wealth.

When the stars of Hollywood leave the broad-line studio corporations, they follow the 80/20 principle. They become single-person businesses for each project. Returns cannot be averaged across a large number of employees and movies. Each movie and each star becomes a separate business. Averages are blown apart.

When Michael Jordan negotiates terms for his participation on the court or ownership of his brand of trainers, he is following the 80/20 principle. He becomes a discrete economic unit and keeps most of the value he personally creates.

When individuals leave Fairchild Semiconductor and start new firms, they are following the 80/20 principle. Fresh variants of old ideas, and smaller, new teams of 80/20 individuals create new value.

The results of following the 80/20 principle are always the same:

- ❖ A new economic entity (or more than one) is created; this can be a new product segment, or a new firm, or a new project.
- ❖ Greater value is created for customers.
- ❖ There is greater selectivity than before: The previous bundle of economic activity is broken into at least two smaller bundles, enabling greater choice and a more accurate reading of preferences for each bundle.
- ❖ There is greater transparency between inputs and outputs: It is easier to see who and what are really producing the greatest value at the lowest relative cost.
- ❖ There is a closer link between value creation and value capture: The individuals and firms that create the greatest value keep a higher share of it. This stimulates greater growth in

the economy, by giving more resources to the most productive units, by encouraging more highly productive individuals and firms to come forward, and by enabling unproductive resources to be redeployed in more valuable ways.

The Irony behind Recent Use of the 80/20 Principle

When the 80/20 principle is taken to its logical conclusion, it undermines the classic large corporation, the typical oligarchy of the mid-twentieth century. There is a certain irony here, however, a certain rough justice.

For most of the twentieth century, the 80/20 principle was largely used by big corporations in order to attain dominant market positions. These corporations saw the logic of a few powerful forces and a mass of weaker ones as being the logic of oligopoly or even of monopoly. Firms focusing on a particular market, using the best forces available to serve that market, ended up with lower costs, more attractive brands, and higher profits, making it very difficult to overturn their dominant market positions. Twenty percent of firms in a market typically ended up with more than 80 percent of it, until just two or three dominant players remained.

In 1976, Bruce Henderson wrote: "All except the two largest-share competitors will either be losers and eventually eliminated or be marginal cash traps reporting profits periodically and reinvesting forever."[2]

Until recently it was generally accepted that the 80/20 principle would favor corporate size and industrial concentration. Yet now it turns out that there is more to competition and definition of business systems than was ever dreamt about in the past. Competition need not be, and increasingly is not, confined to the overall level of activity in the market as a whole. Both activity and the market can be split into many layers and niches.

Are Organizations Deconstructing?

Philip Evans and Thomas S. Wurster of the Boston Consulting Group go further. They herald "the deconstruction of the organization":

> *Decentralized self-organization—the ability of employees to group together, break apart, and regroup across corporate boundaries—will flourish as small companies . . . collaborate with each other. As enterprises learn to do this, they will demonstrate the ability to complete complex projects that had previously been possible only through the hierarchical direction of the large corporations.*
>
> *The ultimate challenge posed by deconstructing supply chains will be to the organization itself. If multiple, smaller organizations can self-organize and collaborate through a pattern of fluid alliances, this raises an interesting question as to why, precisely, the large hierarchical corporation is needed at all.[3]*

Consider the case of Linus Torvalds, a Finnish software designer. In 1991 he invented an operating system he called Linux. He made it freely available on the Web, and invited the IT-heads of the world to debug the system. Linux was developed without capital and, initially, without a corporation. In desktop computers it is miles behind Windows, but by 2000, Linux had taken 31 percent of the Web server market. It is Microsoft's major rival.

Microsoft vice president Paul Maritz put it this way in 1999: "It's almost as though the village blacksmiths of the world can now build axles in their backyard and assemble them together and compete with General Motors. And that's literally what is going on. We have proof through the Linux operating system."[4]

Both Linus Torvalds and Bill Gates are 80/20 individuals. Both have created enormous new value. Neither needed third-party capital. One used a corporation; one didn't. In neither case was a corporation the source of value.

The Importance of Individuals Challenges the
Shareholder Theory of the Firm

What made the corporation valuable to passive outside shareholders was its machinelike characteristics. What made the outside shareholders valuable to the corporation was that building a large, integrated corporation and a large management hierarchy required lots of capital. To insiders and outsiders alike the corporation was a black box. In went capital and out came profits. If the machine produced stable profits it was worth a few years' earnings. If the machine produced growing profits it might be worth 20, 30, or even 50 times earnings.

However, what if the corporation is not a machine? What if it's a vehicle for a few individuals? Specifically, what if the growth—which is what really makes corporations valuable—depends more on individuals and ideas than on the corporate machine? What if Bill Gates is right when he says, "Take away our twenty most important people, and I tell you we would become an unimportant company"?

Then the shareholder theory cannot cope. If 80/20 individuals are more important than capital, a majority of the annual distribution of profits should go to these individuals and not to stockholders. Even more important, it makes no sense to place high value on the corporation if the individuals behind the profits can leave and take the growth prospects of the corporation with them.

Recall the saga of the two 80/20 leaders of PalmPilot and how they ran rings around the corporation that acquired them, setting up a new corporation, Handspring, with the right to license the Palm technology. Similar stories abound. To take two at random, IBM spent $3.5 billion to acquire Lotus Development Corporation, "but more importantly," an analyst wrote, "its chief programmer." I wish IBM luck. At the same time the *Boston Globe* reported that Lucent spent some $900 million buying Nexabit Networks in June 2000, only to see its founder leave within a year, leading several key employees to a new venture opened literally across the street.

If intellectual capital is really more important than the "real" capital frozen in the corporate machine, the "real" capitalists are up a gum tree. One might conclude that, in the search for efficiency and effectiveness, corporations have dug their own graves and those of their financial backers.

If corporations don't do what 80/20 individuals want, the latter can leave and start their own firms. For good ideas and good people, capital will be forthcoming. 80/20 individuals may also be able to ally with the corporations of their choice. What benefits the particular established corporation—an expansion of its profits through alliance with a start-up run by a small team of individuals—may sound the death knell for established corporations as a whole.

The Illogical Theory behind Today's Stock Market

The shareholder theory states that firms go to stock exchanges for capital, which is why passive shareholders should be rewarded with dividends and other ownership rights.

However, Microsoft did not need capital. Founded in 1975 and incorporated in 1981, Microsoft went to the stock exchange only in 1986. With commendable frankness, Microsoft's Michael Brown explains why:

> For pure information age companies . . . when these companies go public, they don't do it to raise proceeds to build plants. They do it to monetize the value of their employee ownership schemes. Microsoft was originally incorporated to create a vehicle to share ownership. . . . And the principal reason we went public was to monetize the value.[5]

"Monetize the value" is a wonderful expression. Put more bluntly, it means that Microsoft listed in order to make Bill Gates and his partners billionaires, and some less exceptional (or newer) employees millionaires. More precisely, the reason was to capitalize these 80/20 individuals' earnings, to place a very high multiple on the value of each year's profits. If Microsoft had been arranged as a partnership, Bill and his chums might still have become billionaires, but they would be poor billionaires, 20 or 30 times poorer than they are.

Perhaps I should not be saying this, but if you stop to think about it, "monetizing the value" of companies is a very odd reason to have a stock market. The reasoning is circular, and works in practice but not at all in theory.

Some 80/20 individuals, like Gates & Co., start a firm. They want to maximize their wealth. They are good at what they do, latch on to powerful business genes, create their own unique variants of new ideas, demonstrate a continual ability to reach the second, third, and subsequent stages of growth by producing yet new variants of success, and create great wealth.

Although some of this wealth is built into the corporate machine, a majority of the wealth-creating ability still emanates from the top individuals in the company. They list on the stock market not because they need capital, but because this is the best way for them to maximize their wealth. If they had not listed, even if they had kept all the profits themselves and not "given some away" to capital, they would not be so rich.

The system works, but only because it directly contradicts the traditional theory of the quoted company. The old theory—which fitted the old practice—was that capital was more important than labor. Because a great deal of capital was needed, the capitalists took the vast majority of the equity in the company, and those who ran the company took little or none. The firm belonged to the owners, and the managers were dispensable hired hands.

In the new practice the firms require little capital and anticipate enormous profits. Therefore, the founders are able to retain a large slug of the equity.

Because they maintain a large share, and because the public markets will multiply annual profits by a large number to arrive at the value of the firm, the founders will want the shares to be quoted. They are motivated by the stock market value of the firm. They want to monetize the value.

If you told 80/20 individuals that they could keep all the profits of the firm each year but that their shares had no other value, they would refuse that deal. 80/20 individuals prefer to have a lower share of the company if it means that the company can be quoted and have a higher value.

222 · THE 80/20 INDIVIDUAL

The practice works only because the capital need pales in comparison to the value of the corporation. If Bill Gates had a very small share in Microsoft, he would benefit from starting another firm with his top twenty people. The value of Microsoft is supported because the stock market knows that Gates has a large share and must protect it. If Microsoft had needed the sort of capital that highly valuable companies used to require, Mr. Gates would have a smaller share, the stock market would know that he and his best people might leave, and the company could never have become so valuable.

Conclusion

One has to ask: Why have a stock market system if it serves no other economic function than to make 80/20 individuals rich? I like the result, but the logic behind it eludes me.

If the stock market did not exist and capital was relatively unimportant compared to individuals, no one could possibly dream up such a system and be taken seriously. It would have all the credibility of a chain letter scam.

That is why, ultimately, I am convinced that our economic system will change. As some 80/20 individuals demand a higher share of today's corporate earnings and others begin their own enterprises, "shareholder value" based on the classic corporation—where ownership and management are separated—will work in neither theory nor practice. Those individuals who generate the wealth will find ways to keep most of it, although increasingly in the form of annual distributions of profits rather than get-rich-quick deals on the stock market. The providers of capital will have to master some other skill, or strike a bargain with individuals who have other skills, to ensure that they select the few investments that will yield high returns to capital after the claims of the individual wealth creators have been met.

There is both justice and market efficiency in the notion of economic individualism. Peter Ustinov quipped that "under capitalism certain people are exploited by other people, whereas under communism it is just the other way round." Under individualism, nobody will be exploited unless they fail to exploit their own abilities to the fullest.

In the long run more wealth will be created as we remove market imperfections blocking the natural flow of wealth to its creators. Yet revolutions are never easy, and the 80/20 revolution may be extremely bumpy. But the rewards are worth the struggle, and it will be up to each of us to take our rightful place on history's winning side.

Notes and References

PART ONE: Turbo-Boost Your Career: Become an 80/20 Individual!

1. How to Be an 80/20 Individual

1. Joseph Moses Juran, *The Quality Control Handbook* (New York: McGraw-Hill, 1951), pp. 38–39. "The economist Pareto found that wealth was non-uniformly distributed in the same way [as Juran noted about quality losses]. Many other instances can be found—the distribution of crime among criminals, the distribution of accidents among hazardous processes, etc. Pareto's principle of unequal distribution applied to distribution of wealth and to distribution of quality losses."

2. Richard Koch, *The 80/20 Principle: The Secret of Achieving More with Less* (London: Nicholas Brealey, 1997; New York: Doubleday Currency, 1998).

3. Ecclesiastes 1:9–10 is worth quoting in full:

   > What has been is what will be,
   > and what has been done is what will be done;
   > and there is nothing new under the sun.
   > Is there a thing of which it is said,
   > "See, this is new"?
   > It has been already,
   > In the ages before us.

4. As Tachi Kiuchi, chairman of Mitsubishi America, says, "A microchip's physical content isn't very valuable. Silica is the cheapest and most abundant raw material on the planet—sand. But a microchip—its shape, its de-

sign, its unseen artistry—is extremely valuable. Yet it comes from a source that seems almost unlimited—the knowledge and inspiration that we draw from the human spirit and mind. This is the most valuable resource, and the most abundant."

2. The Rise of the Creative Individual

1. My account of Keynes's thinking owes much to Professor Skidelsky's landmark biography. See Robert Skidelsky, *John Maynard Keynes: Volume Two, The Economist as Saviour, 1920–1937* (London: Macmillan, 1992), especially p. 335.
2. See Donald L. Laurie, *Venture Catalyst: The Five Strategies for Explosive Corporate Growth* (London: Nicholas Brealey; Cambridge, Mass.: Perseus Publishing, 2001).
3. Charles Handy, *The Elephant and the Flea: Looking Backwards to the Future* (London: Hutchinson, 2001).
4. Robert Johnson, the richest African-American chief executive, founded BET (Black Entertainment Television) in 1985. He recently sold it to Viacom for $2.3 billion in Viacom stock (Viacom also paid $570 million in assuming BET debt). Johnson is an excellent example of an 80/20 leader, driven by his vision.
5. For the best introduction to the subject, see Thomas A. Stewart, *Intellectual Capital: The New Wealth of Organizations* (London: Nicholas Brealey, 1997). The erroneous subtitle says it all: *The truth is that the new and most valuable parts of intellectual capital belong to individuals, not to corporations.*
6. This thought derives from the work of the Boston Consulting Group, which used to be the great advocate of industrial concentration, but which has moved with (or ahead of) the times in advocating the "deconstruction" (blowing up) of monolithic markets by new competitors. See the excellent book by Philip Evans and Thomas S. Wurster, *Blown to Bits: How the New Economics of Information Transforms Strategy* (Boston: Harvard Business School Press, 2000).
7. See Malcolm Gladwell, *The Tipping Point: How Little Things Can Make a Big Difference* (New York: Little Brown, 2000).

PART TWO: The Nine Essentials of 80/20 Success

3. Use Your Most Creative 20 Percent

1. Quoted in Robert Winnett, "Inside the Minds of Britain's Top Bosses," *Sunday Times,* London, July 1, 2001.

2. Michael Maccoby, "Narcissistic Leaders: The Incredible Pros, the Inevitable Cons," *Harvard Business Review* (January–February 2000).
3. Broadly, self-awareness can be increased by three methods. One is to be genuinely open to feedback from the people around you. The second is to organize the feedback process, covering a wide variety of topics in a questionnaire and getting the feedback from as many relevant people as possible. The third is to go through an outside process using a psychological model. For more on self-awareness see chapter 4 of Jonathan Yudelowitz, Richard Koch, and Robin Field, *Smart Things to Know about Leadership* (Oxford: Capstone, 2002).

4. Spawn and Mutate Great Ideas

1. The inventor of the "gene-based" view of life, the view that genes are more fundamental than species or individuals, is Richard Dawkins, the brilliant Oxford biologist. The best account is still Richard Dawkins, *The Selfish Gene*, rev. ed. (Oxford: Oxford University Press, 1989).
2. This is my theory of "business genes," which derives from Richard Dawkins's concept of "memes." A meme is a unit of cultural transmission, like a book, a play, a song, or an idea. A meme is a human artifact, a form of replication peculiar to humans. Memes operate in a way similar to genes.
3. As Richard Dawkins says, "It is not success that makes good genes. It is good genes that make success." See note 1 above.
4. David Hounshell, *From the American System to Mass Production, 1800–1932: The Development of Manufacturing Technology in the United States* (Baltimore: Johns Hopkins University Press, 1984).
5. Charles E. Sorensen with Samuel T. Williamson, *My Forty Years with Ford* (New York: Norton, 1956).
6. Marvin Bower, *The Will to Manage: Corporate Success through Programmed Management* (New York: McGraw-Hill, 1966).

5. Find the Vital Few Profit Sources

1. Robin Field, "Branded Consumer Products," in James Morton, *The Financial Times Global Guide to Investing: The Secrets of the World's Leading Investment Gurus* (London: Financial Times Prentice Hall, 1995), pp. 469–73.
2. See W. Chan Kim and Renée Mauborgne, "Creating New Market Space," *Harvard Business Review* (January–February 1999).
3. See the extremely useful article: W. Chan Kim and Renée Mauborgne, "Value Innovation: The Strategic Logic of High Growth," *Harvard Business Review* (January–February 1997).

4. The calculation that Dell has a 6 percent cost-of-goods advantage comes from Deutsche Morgan Grenfell Technology Group, *The PC Industry* (Deutsche Morgan Grenfell, 1997).

6. Enlist Einstein

1. My focus here has been on how Einstein's theories might be used by entrepreneurs, and in particular how the business gene of time revolution can guide us toward new, unique, valuable businesses. For a fuller account see chapter 7, "On Relativity," in Richard Koch, *The Natural Laws of Business* (New York: Doubleday Currency, 2001).
2. Mark F. Blaxill and Thomas M. Hout, "Make Decisions Like a Fighter Pilot," in Carl W. Stern and George Stalk, Jr., *Perspectives on Strategy* (New York: John Wiley, 1998), p. 165.

7. Hire Great Individuals

1. I am grateful to Geoffrey R. Vautier for pointing out the arithmetic behind the 80/20 principle. Geoff runs the 80/20 Consulting Company Limited in New Zealand. Email: results@the8020co.co.nz.
2. Josef Steindl, *Random Process and the Growth of Firms: A Study of the Pareto Law* (London: Charles Griffin, 1965), p. 18.
3. For those who like algebra, here is Pareto's formula. Call N the number of income earners who receive incomes higher than x, with A and m being the constants. Pareto found that

$$\text{Log } N = \log A + m \log x$$

   Isn't it interesting that the business gene of algebra is often less powerful than that of words, because words are more accessible? If Pareto had expressed his insight in the terms it acquired a generation later—the words expressing the 80/20 principle—he would have had much more influence in his lifetime.
4. Martin Wolf, "Growth Makes the Poor Richer," *Financial Times,* January 24, 2001, p. 17.
5. Lester C. Thurow, *Creating Wealth: The New Rules for Individuals, Companies, and Countries in a Knowledge-Bound Economy* (London: Nicholas Brealey, 1999), chapter 3.
6. Ibid., chapter 10. Thurow's source is the Federal Reserve Board, 1995 data.
7. See Koch, *The 80/20 Principle,* chapters 1 and 13.
8. This is a hint to doctoral students at universities and business schools. The science of success is a powerful business gene, so please start applying academic rigor to it. It is a great way to make your name. Please send a copy of your research to richardjohnkoch@aol.com.

9. Thurow, *Creating Wealth,* chapter 7.

10. There is a great deal of scientific evidence to support the contention that diversity works. See Koch, *The Natural Laws of Business,* chapters 1 and 4. As Charles Darwin observed in *The Origin of Species,* "Unless profitable variations occur, natural selection can do nothing."

11. Except how to sell, a quality that is blithely ignored or undervalued in most strategy consultancies.

12. See chapter 4 of Koch, *The Natural Laws of Business.*

8. *Use Your Current Company to Your Advantage*

1. Assume that the 80/20 person creates a new business after five years with profits of $20 million a year and generates net cash over this period. Value the business on a pretax multiple of 10 and it is worth $200 million. Assume that the 80/20 person is paid $200,000 per annum, or $1 million, over five years. The value created is therefore 200 times the value captured by the individual.

   You can play around with the numbers in different ways. Assume that the individual is very highly valued by the company and that it pays him $1 million a year. That means that he still creates 40 times more value than he receives. Or assume that it is really a team of five equal executives, all paid $200,000 a year, who create the business—each one of them still creates 40 times more value than he or she receives. Whichever way you cut it, 80/20 people who remain employees are underpaid by a huge margin.

2. Quoted in *People Management* (April 19, 2001): 34.

3. Arlyn Tobias Gajilan, "The Parents of the Pilot Try for an Encore with Handspring: A Talk with the Palm Pioneers," *Fortune,* Small Business edition (November 22, 1999; Special Issue/Businessmen of the Century), p. 374.

4. See Sumantra Ghoshal and Christopher A. Bartlett, *The Individualized Corporation* (London: William Heinemann, Random House, 1997). Oddly, there is no definition of the individualized corporation. It is clear, however, that Ghoshal and Bartlett mean a corporation "built on the bedrock of individual initiative at all levels of the company" (chapter 2). There is no hint that individuals may share in ownership. The emphasis is far more on the corporation than on the individual. The authors follow the conventional view that it is corporations rather than individuals that create value: "Companies serve as society's main engine of discovery and progress by continuously creating new value out of the existing endowment of resources" (chapter 10).

9. *Exploit Other Firms*

First epigraph: Karl Marx and Friedrich Engels, *The Communist Manifesto* (1848), chapter 1. I am quoting from the translation by Samuel Moore, first published in 1888, and from the edition with introduction and notes by A. J. P. Taylor (1967, 1985), Penguin Books, p. 86. Marx argues that the conquest of new markets will not create enough demand for the new productive forces of industry, and that there will be progressively more extensive and destructive crises. This did not happen, because the "proletarians" and other poor people eventually provided the market that industry needed. The same redemptive process has happened in every country where free markets have been allowed to operate, and can happen in every poor country that still exists.

Second epigraph: Larry Shulman, *The End of the Public Company—As We Know It* (Boston: Boston Consulting Group, 2000). This is one of BCG's excellent series of "Perspectives." Mr. Shulman may be contacted at shulman.larry@bcg.com. It is ironic that a firm of business consultants that advocates free markets and free enterprise so eloquently should return to Marx's argument after a gap of one and a half centuries. Marx was wrong, but Mr. Shulman is right.

1. Shulman, *The End of the Public Company.*
2. Ibid.: "The globalization wave in many traditional industries is driven more by this specific financial logic than by any compelling strategic imperative. In effect, companies are using their excess cash to take other companies private, thus liquidating the shareholders of the acquired company rather than their own."
3. As late as 1988, an observer at Comdex noted the ambivalence of Microsoft's booth: "While most booths focused on a single blockbuster technology, Microsoft's resembled a Middle Eastern bazaar. In one corner, the company was previewing the second version of Windows . . . in another, it touted its latest release of DOS. Elsewhere, it was displaying OS/2 . . . [and] major new releases of Word, Excel . . . [and] SCO Unix. 'What am I supposed to make of all this?' grumbled a corporate buyer standing next to me." See Eric D. Beinhocker, "On the Origin of Strategies," *McKinsey Quarterly* 4 (1999): 47–57.
4. In the 1980s, IBM's profits averaged between $8 billion and $9 billion per annum. In 1990, IBM made over $10 billion. No firm has ever equaled such profits.
5. See Donald L. Laurie, *Venture Catalyst: The Five Strategies for Explosive Corporate Growth* (London: Nicholas Brealey; Cambridge, Mass.: Perseus Pub-

lishing, 2001). The Corporate Strategy Board and Hewlett-Packard ana-
lyzed the *Fortune* 50 and found that 91 percent of companies reaching that
top group saw their growth drop from previous levels of 9–29 percent down
to 3–4 percent. The study also showed that once companies reach the *Fortune* 10, they always stall. Earnings growth has to come from mergers or
margin improvement.

6. P. R. Milgrom and J. Roberts, *Economics, Organization, and Management*
   (Englewood Cliffs, N.J.: Prentice Hall, 1992).
7. F. A. Hayek, "The Use of Knowledge in Society," *American Economic Review*
   35, no. 4 (1945): 519–30.
8. See M. Granovetter, "The Strength of Weak Ties," *American Journal of Soci-
   ology* 78, no. 6 (1973): 1360–80.

10. Secure Capital

I thank Sir Paul Judge for this epigraph reference. Rutherford uttered
his remark when visited by a team of American scientists, who were
amazed at his cramped work quarters at Cambridge University, England,
and the poor quality of his equipment. Rutherford's point was that in
splitting the atom, thinking from first principles was more important than
having the latest equipment or the plushest laboratory. Ideas dominated
capital.

Following the fall of communism, Western physicists working with their
Russian counterparts were surprised to find that the Russians had much
shorter and neater algorithms. Because the Soviets had much less computer
power, they found ways to make it go further: more from less.

1. See Norman Davies, *Europe: A History* (Oxford: Oxford University Press,
   1996); and Jared Diamond, *Guns, Germs, and Steel: A Short History of
   Everybody for the Last 13,000 Years* (London: Chatto & Windus, 1997).
2. Joseph A. Schumpeter, *Capitalism, Socialism, and Democracy* (New York:
   Harper & Row, 1942).
3. Lester C. Thurow, *Creating Wealth: The New Rules for Individuals, Companies and Countries in a Knowledge-Based Economy* (London: Nicholas
   Brealey, 1999).
4. This is what happened to gold. Once it ceased to outperform other assets,
   it lost its whole rationale. Too much gold and gold was no longer golden.

11. Make Zigzag Progress

1. Sam Walton and John Huey, *Sam Walton: Made in America, My Story* (London: Bantam Books, 1993), p. 53.
2. James Dalton, "What Will Ford Do Next?," *Motor* (May 1926). Numbers from

graph reproduced in Thomas K. McCraw, ed., *Creating Modern Capitalism: How Entrepreneurs, Companies, and Countries Triumphed in Three Industrial Revolutions* (Cambridge, Mass.: Harvard University Press, 1997), p. 283.

3. Alfred D. Chandler, Jr., *Giant Enterprise: Ford, General Motors, and the Automotive Industry* (New York: Harcourt, Brace, & World, 1964), p. 4.

PART THREE: The 80/20 Revolution

12. From Capitalism to Individualism

Epigraph: Peter F. Drucker, *Managing in a Time of Great Change* (London: Butterworth-Heinemann, 1995). The quotation is from the superb 1994 essay, "A Century of Social Transformation," chapter 21 of the book.

1. Adolf A. Berle, Jr., and Gardiner C. Means, *The Modern Corporation and Private Property* (New York: Macmillan, 1932).

2. Alfred D. Chandler, *The Visible Hand: The Managerial Revolution in American Business* (Cambridge, Mass.: Belknap Press of Harvard University Press, 1977).

3. Author's analysis based on *Fortune,* April 16, 2001. The ownership percentages are taken from the 2001 proxy statements of Berkshire Hathaway, Microsoft, and Wal-Mart.

4. I invite a doctoral student or a consulting firm to calculate the percentage of market value accruing to individual-centered corporations over time, using different definitions. It would be particularly revealing to see a very-long-time series, from the start of the Dow-Jones index to today. For the most liberal definition, including companies where an executive has become a billionaire at today's values, one should of course adjust for inflation in calculating the cutoff point in each year. I also invite *Fortune* to include in its rankings an identification of individual-centered corporations, using whatever definition it considers most appropriate.

13. What If?

Epigraph quoted in Stewart, *Intellectual Capital.*

1. See Shulman, *The End of the Public Company.*

2. See Paul Wallace, *Agequake* (London: Nicholas Brealey, 1999).

Appendix

1. Quoted in *Wharton Alumni Magazine* (winter 2000): 10.

2. Bruce Henderson quoted in Carl W. Stern and George Stalk, Jr., *Perspectives on Strategy* (New York: John Wiley, 1998).

3. Philip Evans and Thomas S. Wurster, *Blown to Bits* (Boston: Harvard Business School Press, 2000).
4. *United States of America v. Microsoft Corporation et alia*, Washington D.C., January 26, 1999, pp. 60–61.
5. Quoted in Stewart, *Intellectual Capital*, p. 105.

Acknowledgments

I owe a huge debt to Dr. Marcus Alexander of the Ashridge Strategic Management Center. His work on how corporate boundaries are shifting played a major part in convincing me that capitalism is giving way to a new economic system. Originally, we collaborated on a book to be co-authored, and there are strong traces of Marcus's thinking throughout Part Three of this book. Having said that, I have gone further in drawing conclusions than Marcus would have done, so blame me and not him if you disagree.

My second obligation is to "Rachel," a friend and former colleague. She is flesh and blood, alive and well, disguised but easily decoded by her circle, and I am also grateful for her willingness to bare her soul in print.

Next, I have pleasure in paying tribute to all the 80/20 individuals (more than sixty in total) featured in this book—especially those friends still living who gave their permission for their inclusion. I do not mean that I have been bumping off recalcitrant individuals, just that some are public figures already.

I very much appreciate the editorial efforts of Nicholas Brealey, Sue Coll, and especially Sally Lansdell, and, for this American edition, huge praise is due to Roger Scholl, Sarah Rainone, and Stephanie Land. I have been very lucky in the skill, insight, and line-by-line editing provided by Sarah, Stephanie, Roger, and the entire Currency Doubleday team. My great thanks are also due to my friend and former business partner, Jim Lawrence, who provided two of the freshest and most intriguing examples of 80/20 individuals in the whole book.

Finally, praise be to Vilfredo Pareto, who set the ball rolling in the first place. My ambition is to see Pareto firmly replace Marx as the most appreciated economist and sociologist of the nineteenth century. Marx gave us capitalism, but Pareto gave us the 80/20 principle, and indirectly, individualism, an economy that is replacing capitalism and may well last a great deal longer, and have even more awesome results.

Index

Page numbers of illustrations appear in italics.

Absolut Vodka, 139–40
Accenture, 20, 209
Agequake (Wallace), 232n. 2
agricultural revolutions, 10, 175, 176
Allen, Paul, 208
Allied Domecq, 139–40, 143, 146
Allied Lyons, 139
Amazon.com, 59, 181
American Telephone and Telegraph, 176
Animal Farm (Orwell), 208
Anthem (Rand), 208
AOL Time Warner, 182
Apple Computer, 73–74, 181, 182
Archimedes, 13
Arthur D. Little, 51
automobile industry
  market, 25
  market capitalism and, 177–78, 232n. 3
  Model T Ford, 48–49, 177

Bain Capital, 74
Bain & Company, 44, 52, 53, 59, 72, 120, 121
Bain, Bill, 52, 72, 105–6, 108, 120–21

Bains, Gurnek, 32
Barlett, Christopher A., 229n. 4
BBC (British Broadcasting Company), 39
BBC Online, 40
Bear Stearns, 40
Beefeater, 139–40
Belgo, 86–87, *88*, 89, 91–92, 168–69
Benhamou, Eric, 124
Berkshire Hathaway, 20, 181, 232n. 3
Berle, Adolf, 176, 182, 207, 232n. 1
Betfair, 61–62
Bezos, Jeff, 32, 181
Bierodromes, 168–69
Birt, John, 39, 40
Bjorn-Ingvar, 36–37
Black Entertainment Television, 23, 226n. 4
Blais, Denis, 91
Blaxill, Mark F., 228n. 2
Blown to Bits (Evans and Wurster), 226n. 6, 233n. 3
BMW, 73
Boscariol, Olivo, 38–39
Boston Consulting Group (BCG), 44, 51, 52, 72, 89, 108, 119–20, 122–24, 130, 135, 136, 193, 210, 218, 226n. 6
Boston Safe and Deposit Company, 119–20, 123, 130

Bower, Marvin, 51, 57, 121, 227n. 6
Bowie, David, 208
"Branded Consumer Products" (Field),
    227n. 1
branded goods, 137–38
Branson, Richard, 181
Brimley, Wilfred
Brown, Michael, 220
Buffett, Warren, 20, 100, 181
Burnham, James, 207
business enterprises
    capital for, securing, 149–61
    case study, betting, 59–62
    cash, and success of, 155
    characteristics of successful ideas, 50
    choke points, 145
    computer development as example, 46
    consulting, as models for the future,
        119
    developing, mutating great ideas, 57–59
    80/20 frugality principle and, 145
    80/20 individuals, advantage over
        corporations, 147–48
    80/20 individuals as heart of, 89
    equity, demise of importance, 197–99
    experimentation, at second stage, 166–71
    exploiting other firms to start, 138–48
    expropriating the owners, 119–20
    Ford and mass production example, 49
    formula, 46
    "genes," 47, 51–56, 98–101, 227n. 2
    Go-Gurt, 56
    hotel market, 54–56
    how to build your 80/20 business, 126–31
    hybrid, individual-centered, 125–26,
        129–31
    as ideas, 45–46
    incubator deals, 116–19
    infrastructure available for, 137–38, 179
    local knowledge, 143–44, 147
    management consulting, evolution, 50–54
    Microsoft example, 140–41
    missing markets, identifying, 143–45
    niches, 136
    ownership of firms, 120–22
    Plymouth Gin example, 139–40
    profits, remodeling for, 65–82
    second stage of growth, 163–71
    self-service idea, 47

    start-ups within existing corporations, 63,
        117–18, 125–26, 159
    subcontracting, 136
    third party deals, 146
    time, factoring in, 83–93
    the vital few, 47–48

capital, 149–61
    capital providers as partners, 160–61
    cash, excess in corporations, 136–37
    cash, as king, 195–97
    cash, obsession with, 160
    decline of, theoretical, 199, 220
    difficulty of raising, 155
    80/20 individuals, raising of, 152–53, 195
    excess, using, 139–40
    growth and capital investments, 153–55
    keeping score with, 161
    individualism and, 181, 184
    multiplying and cash-to-cash ratio,
        155–57
    private equity, 154, 208
    providing one's own, 157–58
    raising more than needed, 157
    recapitalizations, 193–94
    reducing amount needed, 145, 157
    returns on, historical, 151, 152, 180–81
    sources for, 158–60, 195, 213
    three lessons from Columbus, 150–51
    using another firm's, 145
    See also venture capital
capitalism, 152–53, 222
    demise of, 199
    individualism vs., 175, 179–87, 187,
        208–10
    invisible hand, 178
    managerial, 176–79, 206–10
    market, 176, 186, 187
    milestones in rise of managerial
        capitalism, 206–7 (Table 1)
    Capitalism, Socialism and Democracy
        (Schumpeter), 231n. 2
Cappelli, Peter, 214
Carnegie, Andrew, 16, 49, 182, 184, 206
cash-to-cash ratio, 155–57, 197
Caven, Niall, 56, 91
Champy, James, 45
Chandler, Alfred D., Jr., 232n. 1, 232n. 3
Chohan brothers, 77–79

Churchill, Winston, 205
Clark, Jim
Coca-Cola, 78–79, 183
Collischon, David, 62, 167
Columbus, Christopher, 16, 149–50, 151
Comdex, 230n. 3
communism, 222
Communist Manifesto, The, 230n.
   (epigraph)
computer
   as business idea, 46
   Dell and, 76, 228n. 4
   Jobs and personal computer, 73–74
   microchip, and birth of an idea, 9, 225n. 4
"Core Competence of the Corporation,
   The" (Prahalad and Hamel), 209
Corporate Strategy Board, 230–31n. 5
corporations
   case study, management, 34–36, 63–64,
     79–80, 112–13
   case study, managers at PepsiCo, 77–79
   cash excess in, 136–37
   core business and focus, 208–9
   creativity in, and setting, 36
   demise of, 190–203
   80/20, 210–11, 214–17
   80/20 hybrid deal, 124–25, 129–31
   80/20 individuals in, 24–25, 62–63,
     115–33
   80/20 principle in, 25–26
   four elements in shift to managerial
     capitalism, 178
   growth, 142
   hiring great individuals, 95–113
   how to exploit for start-ups, 143–47
   incubator deals in, 116–19, 125–26, 159
   individual-centered, 181–84, 232n. 3
   individuals vs., 18–20, 179–81
   LBOs and LBIs, 193, 208
   managerial capitalism and large, 175,
     176–78, 206–8
   market value, 182
   mergers and acquisitions, 19, 54, 142
   milestones in the decline of managerial
     capitalism, 208–10 (Table 2)
   milestones in rise of managerial
     capitalism, 206–7 (Table 1)
   monetization, fall of, 191–93, 220
   monopoly of enterprises within, 212–13

   mutation into "incubating" firms, 190–91
   open-ended deals with, 142–48
   overproduction in, 135, 136–38, 231n. 3
   private buyouts of, 193–94
   recapitalizations, 193–94
   revenues vs. profits in, 136
   shareholder theory, 219–20, 222
   starting businesses within, 63, 117–18,
     125–26, 159
creativity or creation
   breakthroughs, thought, and
     experimentation, 10
   business innovation and value, 10
   as collision of ideas and individuals, 10
   80/20 individual and, 14, 16–18
   80/20 principle and, 8–10, 17, 18
   rearranging things that already exist, 9
   second stage of growth and, 163–71
   setting for, 36
   seven themes for new products or
     services, 73–77
   20 percent spike and, 32–36
"Creating New Market Space" (Kim and
   Mauborgne), 227n. 2
Creating Wealth (Thurow), 228n. 5, 228n. 6,
   229n. 9, 231n. 3
Cruise, Tom, 185
customers
   grading, 70
   highest ration of value to cost, 72–73
   identifying most profitable, 70–73

Dalton, James, 231n. 2
Darwin, Charles, 16, 229n. 10
Davies, Norman, 231n. 1
Dawkins, Richard, 227n. 1, 227n. 2, 227n. 3
Dell Corporation, 76, 211, 228n. 4
Deutsche Morgan Grenfell, 228n. 4
Diamond, Jared, 231n. 1
Domino's Pizza, 74
Drucker, Peter, 175, 208, 209, 232n.
   (epigraph)
Dubinsky, Donna, 124–25, 192

Easyjet, 76
eBay, 59
Ecclesiastes 1:9–10, 9, 225n. 3
Economics, Organization, and Management
   (Milgrom and Roberts), 231n. 6

80/20 frugality principle, 145
80/20 individual
  as billionaire, 23
  business choice, most profitable markets,
    135–36
  case studies, management, 34–36, 59–64,
    77–80, 112–13
  compensation for, 189
  control, desire for, 8
  corporations and, 18–20, 115–33,
    189–203
  creativity and, 16–18
  entrepreneurs as, 15, 125–33
  examples of, 14–15, 16, 36–40
  "fleas and elephants," 22
  individualism and, 181–87
  leaving or staying with your company,
    115–16, 192
  in organizations, 7–8, 89–90, 115–33
  partnership model for, 123–24
  personal vs. organizational power, 15,
    181–84
  rise of, 184–86
  second stage of growth and, 163–71
  as team-based individualism, 13–14, 16,
    20–22, 43–44
  time, use of and, 93
  "20 percent spike," 32–36, 40–43, 91
  outsourcing and, 33, 145
  value of, to organization, 95–97
  as wealth creators, 20, 23, 26–27, 97–99
  wealth transfers to, 187
80/20 principle, 5, 6
  as business tool, 6
  capital and, 150–51
  computer as example, 46
  creative individuals and, 16–18, 170–71
  de-averaging returns, 213, 215
  division of markets and, 180
  Filofax strategy and, 167
  history, 4–5
  identifying profit sources with, 65–82
  individual fulfillment and, 6
  individual wealth creation and, 98
  irony behind, 217
  new synthesis of theory and, 210–12
  time and, 84–93
  20 percent of the 20 percent, 46, 58–59
  value creation by, 214–17

80/20 Principle, The (Koch), 3, 6, 25, 225n.
    2, 228n. 7
80/20 revolution, 175–87, 187
  decline in stock market and, 205–6
  division of markets and, 180
  four key elements, 179–80
  individualism and, 180, 186–87, 205–6
  societal consequences of, 200, 201–4
Einstein, Albert, 16, 17, 83, 84, 100, 228n. 1
Elephant and the Flea, The (Handy), 22,
    226n. 3
Elliott, Robert K., 189, 232n. (epigraph)
Ellison, Larry, 181
employees
  appreciate young talent, 103–5
  compensation for wealth creators, 104,
    115
  excess of, and availability, 138
  exploit the theory of wealth/talent
    arbitrage, 102–3
  fun and friendship, 106–7
  hiring, 95–113
  hiring talent vs. mediocrity, 101
  holding out for best deal, 118–19
  incubator deals and, 116–18
  leaving or staying with company, 115–16
  locking in great people, 105–7
  long-term employees, 103–4
  mezzanine layer, 121–22
  patron/protégé relationship, 111–12
  recruitment, sources for, 104
  stock option plan (ESOP), 120
  talent, compensation for, 103
  theory of the tribe, 109–10
  value of oddballs (diversity), 108
  venture DNA and, 110–11
  virtuous cycle, 107, 122
  vital few, identifying, 69–70
  what to do if great employees leave, 107
"End of the Public Company, The"
    (Shulman), 230n. (epigraph), 230n. 1,
    230n. 2, 232n. 1
Engels, Friedrich, 135, 230n. (epigraph)
entrepreneurs
  capital and, 154–61
  80/20 individual as, 15
  80/20 revolution and, 179–80
  host/profit-sharing solution, 125–26
  incubator solution, 126

MBOs and, 112–13, 127–29
partnership structure and, 125
Schumpeter on, 153
second stage of growth and, 163–71
team assistance and, 20–21
Europe (Davies), 231n. 1
Evans, Iain, 44, 106
Evans, Philip, 218, 226n. 6, 233n. 3

Fairchild Semiconductor, 216
Federal Computer Week, 63
Field, Robin, 68–69, 167, 227n. 1, 227n. 3
Filofax, 62, 68–69, 167–68
Flutter.com, 61–62
Focus (Ries), 209–10
Ford, Harrison, 185
Ford, Henry, 16, 49, 166, 177, 182, 184, 206
Ford Motor Company, 49–50, 177
  Model T, 48–49
  second stage of growth, 166–67, 231n. 2,
    232n. 3
Formule 1, 75
Forster, E. M., 163
Fortune
  20, 183
  50, growth among, 19, 142
  500, 181, 182, 183, 209
Fountainhead, The (Rand), 208
Freud, Sigmund, 32
*From the American System to Mass
  Production, 1800–1932* (Hounshell),
  227n. 4
Fuller, Thomas, 65

Gajilan, Arlyn Tobias, 229n. 3
Gates, Bill, 3, 16, 19–20, 23, 32, 39, 100,
  140–41, 181, 192, 208, 218, 219, 220,
  222
GE Capital, 191
General Electric (GE), 183, 194
General Mills, 56
Ghoshal, Sumantra, 229n. 4
Giant Enterprise (Chandler), 232n. 3
Gladwell, Malcolm, 26, 226n. 8
Goizuetta, Robert, 183
Goldman Sachs, 23, 120, 181
Granovetter, M., 231n. 7
Greenspan, Alan, 154
Grove, Andy, 32, 115, 181

growth
  corporate, 142
  corporate, profit sources and, 66
  GDP, 154
  economy and small companies, 19
  Fortune 50 and, 19, 142
  historic, 151, 154
  intellectual capital as essence of, 138
  in management consulting, 53–54
  mergers and acquisitions, 19, 142, 167–68
  second stage of, 163–71
  underinvestment as enemy of, 15
  U.S. economy, 66, 154
  value and, 7
  Yoplait and Go-Gurt, 56
"Growth Makes the Poor Richer" (Wolf),
  228n. 4
Guns, Germs, and Steel (Diamond), 231n. 1

Haller, Rick, 117–18, 130, 131
Hamel, Gary, 209
Hamlet (Shakespeare), 31
Handspring, 124–25, 192, 219, 229n. 3
Handy, Charles, 22, 226n. 3
Hanks, Tom, 185
Hannah, Josh, 59–62
Harley-Davidson, 73
Hawkins, Jeff, 124–25, 192
Hayek, F. A., 143, 208, 231n. 7
Henderson, Bruce Doolin, 51–52, 57, 108,
  119–20, 217, 232n. 2
Hewlett-Packard, 181
Hitler, Adolf, 207
Hollywood and stars, 185, 208, 216
Honda, 73, 74
Hounshell, David, 48, 227n. 4
Hout, Thomas M., 228n. 1
Hugo, Victor, 45

IBM, 140–41, 219, 230n. 4
idea(s)
  business enterprises as, 45–46
  business formula, 46
  business genes, 47, 50–56, 98–101, 227n. 2
  case study, betting, 59–62
  characteristics contributing to success, 50
  combine and tweak previous, 49
  competition between, 48
  creativity and individuals, 10

enlisting, mutating business ideas, 57–59
management consulting, 50–54
successful, demise of, 48–49
time as value creation, 86–87, *88*, 89
transparency of, 213
uniqueness of, six factors, 58
the vital few, 47
as "wealth creation multiple," 17
Ikea, 76
incubator deals, 116–19, 125–26, 159,
    190–91
individualism, 175–87, *187*, 208, 222
companies, private, vs. corporations, 190
decline in managerial capitalism and rise
    of, 208–10 (table 2)
individual-centered corporation,
    181–84
reversal of managerial capitalism, 179–80
rise of 80/20 individuals, 184–86
Individualized Corporation, The (Ghoshal
    and Barnett), 229n. 4
Industrial Revolution, 175, 176, 186, *187*
"Inside the Minds of Britain's Top Bosses"
    (Winnett), 226n. 1
Intel, 26, 190
intellectual capital, 7, 23–25, 131–33, 184,
    210, 219–20
Intellectual Capital (Stewart), 226n. 5, 232n.
    (epigraph), 233n. 5
internal rate of return (IRR), 155–57, 197
International Data Group, 63
Internet
    case study, 59–62
    as electronic marketplace, 59
    floating e-business sectors of firms, 121
    virtual corporations, 210

Jobs, Steve, 32, 73–74, 181
John Maynard Keynes (Skidelsky), 226n. 1
Johnson & Johnson, 190, 194
Johnson, Robert, 23, 226n. 4
Jones, Barry, 120, 122–23, 130
Jordan, Michael, 185, 216
Judge, Sir Paul, 231n. (epigraph)
Juran, Joseph Moses, 4, 225n. 1

Keynes, John Maynard, 15–16, 226n. 1
Kim, W. Chan, 227n. 2, 227n. 3
Kiuchi, Tachi, 225n. 4

Koch, Richard, 3, 6, 227n. 3, 228n. 1, 228n.
    7, 229n. 10
Belgo, 86–89, 168–69
Filofax, 167–68
identifying profit sources and, 67–68
Law of Individual Wealth Creation,
    97–98
management consulting business (LEK),
    44, 52–53, 69–70, 121
patron/protégé relationship, 111–12
Plymouth Gin and, 139–40
20 percent spike of, 44
website, 228n. 8
Zoffany hotels, 54–56, 135–36, 169–70
Kroc, Ray, 62

labor, 145. *See also* outsourcing;
    subcontracting
Landmann, Fritz, 63
Laurie, Donald L., 226n. 2, 230n. 5
Lawrence, Jim, 44, 106
Lazarus, Charles, 62
LBOs (leveraged buyouts), 193, 208
leadership, 32, 91, 227n. 2
LEK Consulting, 53–54, 69–73, 77, 106,
    111–12, 121, 142
Lenin, Vladimir Ilyich, 206–7
Liberation Movement (Peters), 209
Libra Bank, 117–18
Libris Media AB, 37
Linux, 218
Lotus Development Corporation,
    219
Lucent, 219
Lutz, Scott, 56
Lynx, 40

Maccoby, Michael, 32, 227n. 2
"Make Decisions Like a Fighter Pilot"
    (Blaxill and Hout), 228n. 1
management buyout (MBO), 112–13,
    127–29
management case study
    business genes and, 131–33
    exploiting other firms by, 142
    as original, mutated idea, 63–64
    profit sources, identifying, 79–80
    time, as value source, 92–93
    20 percent spike, finding, 34–36

undercompensation of, 112–13, 115, 229n. 1
management consulting, 229n. 11
  evolution of, 50–54
  as models for the future, 119
  profit and, 80–81
  See also specific firms
managers
  in collaborating firms, 146–47
  decline in importance of, 214
  holding out for best deal, 118–19
  incubator deals for, 116–19
  leaving or staying with your company, 115–16
  managerial capitalism, 175, 177–78, 206–10
  reduced need for, 184
  theory of the tribe and, 109–10
Managerial Revolution, The (Burnham), 207
Managing in a Time of Great Change (Drucker), 232n. (epigraph)
Maritz, Paul, 218
Mars, Forrest and John, 182
Marx, Karl, 135, 152, 153, 230n. (epigraph)
Matsushita, Konosuke, 16
Mauborgne, Renée, 227n. 2, 227n. 3
McDonald's, 62
McGovern, Pat, 63
McKinsey & Company, Inc., 44, 50–51, 52, 57, 120–21
McKinsey, James O., 51
McLuhan, Marshall, 83
Means, Gardiner, 176, 182, 207, 232n. 1
memes, 227n. 2
mergers and acquisitions (M&A), 19
  Filofax and, 167–68
  LEK and, 54, 77
Microsoft, 19–20, 23, 26, 77, 140–41, 179–80, 181, 191–92, 208, 209, 210, 211, 220, 222, 230n. 3, 232n. 3, 233n. 4
Milgrom, P. R., 231n. 6
Mill, John Stuart, 21
"missing markets," 143–45
Mitsubishi America, 225n. 4
Modern Corporation and Private Property (Berle and Means), 176, 207, 232n. 1
Monical, Vince, 59–62
Morita, Akio, 16
Murphy, John, 140

My Forty Years with Ford (Sorensen), 227n. 5

"Narcissistic Leaders" (Maccoby), 227n. 2
Natural Laws of Business, The (Koch), 228n. 1, 229n. 10, 229n. 12
Newton, Isaac, 16
Nexabit Networks, 219
niche markets, 136
Nike, 77, 185, 211
1984 (Orwell), 208
Norton [motorcycles], 73

Oracle, 23, 181
Origin of Species, The (Darwin), 229n. 10
Orwell, George, 208
outsourcing, 209
  capital, reducing need for and, 157, 158
  individualism and, 184
  non-profitable sectors, 140, 145
  personal, 32–33

PA Consulting, 142
PalmPilot, 124–25, 192, 219, 229n. 3
Pareto, Vilfredo, 4, 97, 225n. 1, 228n. 3, 235–36
Pareto principle, 5–6, 84
partners
  capital providers as, 160–61
  compensation for, 105–6, 121–24, 229n. 1
  80/20 individuals as, 123–24, 125
  ideal number, 110
  need for, 82, 110
  rise of, 200–201
  temporary vs. permanent, 146
  as vital few, 69
partnership, professional, 120–22
PC Industry, The (Deutsche Morgan Grenfell), 228n. 4
PepsiCo, 77–79
Peters, Tom, 209
Plisnier, André, 91–92
Plymouth Gin, 139–40, 143, 146
"power of weak ties," 147, 231n. 8
Prahalad, C. K., 209
price/earnings ratio, 193–94, 196
Procter & Gamble, 78, 190
profit, 65–82
  consulting industry, analysis, 80–81

customers and, 70–73
80/20 frugality principle and, 145
Filofax overhaul, 68–69
finding the vital few profit sources, 66–69
products and services, 73–77
sweet spots, identifying, 77
time, product- and service-, 83–93
vital few employees or partners, 69–70

Quality Control Handbook, The (Juran), 4, 225n. 1

Rand, Ayn, 208
Random Process and the Growth of Firms (Steindl), 228n. 2
Reeve, Jamie, 39
retailers
branded goods and, 137–38
self-service, 85–86
Wal-Mart, 164–65
Ries, Al, 209
Road to Serfdom, The (Hayek), 208
Roberts, J., 231n. 6
Rockefeller, John D., 182
Roddick, Anita, 181
Rolls, Charles, 140
"Rule of the Vital Few," 4, 225n. 1
Rutherford, Ernest, 149, 231n. (epigraph)
Ryanair, 76

Saint Gobain, 38
Sam Walton (Walton and Huey), 231n. 1
Schumpeter, Joseph, 153, 231n. 2
Seagate Technologies, 193
Selfish Gene, The (Dawkins), 227n. 1
Shakespeare, William, 31
Shaw, George Bernard, 33
Shulman, Larry, 135, 136–37, 193, 230n. (epigraph), 230n. 1, 230n. 2, 232n. 1
website, 230n. (epigraph)
Sinha, Suman, 77–79
Skidelsky, Robert, 226n. 1
Smart Things to Know About Leadership (Yudelowitz, Koch, and Field), 227n. 3
Sonley, Nick, 56, 91
Sorensen, Charles, 49, 227n. 5
Soros, George, 181
Southwest Airlines, 76
Spielberg, Steven, 185

sports industry, 185, 208
Steindl, Josef, 97, 228n. 2
Stewart, Thomas A., 226n. 5, 232n. (epigraph), 233n. 5
stock market
baby boomers and investment in, 196–97
cash as king vs., 193–94
decline in share prices, prediction, 205
monetization and, 191–93, 220–21
shareholder theory, 219–20, 222
theoretical fall of, 190, 199–200
valuation, 192–93, 197
subcontracting, 136, 211. *See also* outsourcing

teams, 13–14, 16, 20–22
80 percent and need for, 43, 44
emotional support from, 43
theory of the tribe, 109–10
venture DNA and, 110–11
3Com, 124, 125
Thurow, Lester, 154, 228n. 5, 228n. 6, 229n. 9, 231n. 3
time
case study, manager, 92–93
compressing delivery time, 84–87
detailed plan to cut, 87, 88, 89
just-in-time manufacturing, 87
product-, 84
relativity and, 83
self-service, 85–86
service-, 84
subject to 80/20 principle, 89–92
"tipping point," 26, 226n. 7
Torvalds, Linus, 218
Toyota, 75
Toys 'R' Us, 62
Triumph company, 73
Trust House Forte, 144
"20 percent spike," 32–34
business idea and, 50, 91
core competencies and, 91–92
examples, 34–40
identifying, 40–41, 227n. 3
leadership and, 32, 91, 227n. 2
new ventures and, 42–43
questionnaire, 40–41
working on, 42

"Use of Knowledge in Society, The"
(Hayek), 231n. 7
U.S. economy, 66, 97, 154
U.S. Robotics, 124
U.S. Steel, 206
Ustinov, Peter, 222

value
business innovation and, 10
business growth and, 7
80/20 principle and, 214–17
innovation and, 75–76, 163–71, 227n. 3
returns on capital, 149–50, 151, 163
time, using to create value, 83–93
"Value Innovation" (Kim and Mauborgne),
227n. 3
Vangal Ramash, 77–79
Vautier, Geoffrey R., 228n. 1
venture capital, 154, 158, 159–60, 161, 179,
208
cash-to-cash ratio, 155, 197
80/20 individuals backed by, 195
equity, demise of importance, 197–99
IRR and, 155–57, 197
Venture Catalyst (Laurie), 226n. 2, 230n. 5
Viacom, 226n. 4
Vin & Sprit, 139–40, 146
Virgin, 40, 181, 213
Visible Hand, The (Chandler), 232n. 1
"vital few," 47–48
customers, most profitable, 70–73
employees or partners, 69–70
products and services, 73–77
profit sources, finding, 65–82

"Rule of the Vital Few," 4
short-listing ideas, 57

Wallace, Paul, 232n. 2
Wal-Mart, 164–65, 181, 182, 232n. 3
Walton, Sam, 16, 164–65, 182, 231n. 1
wealth creation
appreciate young talent, 103–5
"business genes" and, 98–102, 227n. 2
changes in nature of, 205–6
80/20 individual and, 20, 23, 26–27
80/20 principle and, 98
hiring talent, 101
Koch's Law of Individual, 97–98
luck and, 99
multiple, 98–99
new sources of, 213
talent and, 97, 99–101
theory of wealth/talent arbitrage, 102–3
Welch, Jack, 32, 183
Whitbread, 139
Will to Manage, The (Bower), 227n. 6
Winfrey, Oprah, 14, 181
Winnett, Robert, 226n. 1
Wolf, Martin, 228n. 4
Wurster, Thomas S., 218, 226n. 6, 233n. 3

Yoplait, 56
YSC, 32
Yudelowitz, Jonathan, 227n. 3

Zoffany Hotels, 54–56, 91, 135–36, 144
formula, 55–56
Mark II, 169–70

© Mike Goldwater

ABOUT THE AUTHOR

An extraordinarily successful entrepreneur RICHARD KOCH is the bestselling author of *The 80/20 Principle*. His ventures have included consulting for hotels, restaurants, personal organizers, and the distilling industry. A former consultant with the Boston Consulting Group and former partner of Bain & Company, he currently lives in London, England.